JAMESTOWN EDUCATION

Timed Readings Plus *in Science*

25 Two-Part Lessons
with Questions for
Building Reading Speed and Comprehension

BOOK 2

Glencoe McGraw-Hill

New York, New York   Columbus, Ohio   Chicago, Illinois   Peoria, Illinois   Woodland Hills, California

JAMESTOWN EDUCATION

Glencoe/McGraw-Hill

A Division of The McGraw·Hill Companies

ISBN: 0-07-827371-4

Copyright © The McGraw-Hill Companies, Inc. All rights reserved. Except as per-
mitted under the United States Copyright Act of 1976, no part of this publication
may be reproduced or distributed in any form or by any means, or stored in a
database or retrieval system, without prior written permission of the publisher.

Send all queries to:
Glencoe/McGraw-Hill
8787 Orion Place
Columbus, OH 43240-4027

3 4 5 6 7 8 9 10 021 08 07 06 05 04 03

CONTENTS

To the Student

You probably talk at an average rate of about 150 words a minute. If you are a reader of average ability, you read at a rate of about 250 words a minute. So your reading speed is nearly twice as fast as your speaking or listening speed. This example shows that reading is one of the fastest ways to get information.

The purpose of this book is to help you increase your reading rate and understand what you read. The 25 lessons in this book will also give you practice in reading science articles and in preparing for tests in which you must read and understand nonfiction passages within a certain time limit.

Reading Faster and Better

Following are some strategies that you can use to read the articles in each lesson.

Previewing

Previewing before you read is a very important step. This helps you to get an idea of what a selection is about and to recall any previous knowledge you have about the subject. Here are the steps to follow when previewing.

Read the title. Titles are designed not only to announce the subject but also to make the reader think. Ask yourself questions such as What can I learn from the title? What thoughts does it bring to mind?

What do I already know about this subject?

Read the first sentence. If they are short, read the first two sentences. The opening sentence is the writer's opportunity to get your attention. Some writers announce what they hope to tell you in the selection. Some writers state their purpose for writing; others just try to get your attention.

Read the last sentence. If it is short, read the final two sentences. The closing sentence is the writer's last chance to get ideas across to you. Some writers repeat the main idea once more. Some writers draw a conclusion—this is what they have been leading up to. Other writers summarize their thoughts; they tie all the facts together.

Skim the entire selection. Glance through the selection quickly to see what other information you can pick up. Look for anything that will help you read fluently and with under-standing. Are there names, dates, or numbers? If so, you may have to read more slowly.

Reading for Meaning

Here are some ways to make sure you are making sense of what you read.

Build your concentration. You cannot understand what you read if you are not concentrating. When you discover that your thoughts are straying, correct the situation right away. Avoid distractions and distracting situations. Keep in mind the information you learned from previewing. This will help focus your attention on the selection.

Read in thought groups. Try to see meaningful combinations of words—phrases, clauses, or sentences. If you look at only one word at a time (called word-by-word reading), both your comprehension and your reading speed suffer.

Ask yourself questions. To sustain the pace you have set for yourself and to maintain a high level of concentration and comprehension, ask yourself questions such as What does this mean? or How can I use this information? as you read.

Finding the Main Ideas

The paragraph is the basic unit of meaning. If you can quickly discover and understand the main idea of each paragraph, you will build your comprehension of the selection.

Find the topic sentence. The topic sentence, which contains the main idea, often is the first sentence of a paragraph. It is followed by sentences that support, develop, or explain the main idea. Sometimes a topic sentence comes at the end of a paragraph. When it does, the supporting details come first, building the base for the topic sentence. Some paragraphs do not have a topic sentence; all of the sentences combine to create a meaningful idea.

Understand paragraph structure. Every well-written paragraph has a purpose. The purpose may be to inform, define, explain or illustrate. The purpose should always relate to the main idea and expand on it. As you read each paragraph, see how the body of the paragraph tells you more about the main idea.

Relate ideas as you read. As you read the selection, notice how the writer puts together ideas. As you discover the relationship between the ideas, the main ideas come through quickly and clearly.

Mastering Reading Comprehension

Reading fast is not useful if you don't remember or understand what you read. The two exercises in Part A provide a check on how well you have understood the article.

Recalling Facts

These multiple-choice questions provide a quick check to see how well you recall important information from the article. As you learn to apply the reading strategies described earlier, you should be able to answer these questions more successfully.

Understanding Ideas

These questions require you to think about the main ideas in the article. Some main ideas are stated in the article; others are not. To answer some of the questions, you need to draw conclusions about what you read.

The five exercises in Part B require multiple answers. These exercises provide practice in applying comprehension and critical-thinking skills that you can use in all your reading.

Recognizing Words in Context

Always check to see whether the words around an unfamiliar word—its context—can give you a clue to the word's meaning. A word generally appears in a context related to its meaning.

Suppose, for example, that you are unsure of the meaning of the word *expired* in the following passage:

> Vera wanted to check out a book, but her library card had expired. She had to borrow my card, because she didn't have time to renew hers.

You could begin to figure out the meaning of *expired* by asking yourself a question such as, What could have happened to Vera's library card that would make her need to borrow someone else's card? You might realize that if Vera had to renew her card, its usefulness must have come to an end or run out. This would lead you to conclude that the word *expired* must mean "to come to an end" or "to run out." You would be right. The context suggested the meaning.

Context can also affect the meaning of a word you already know. The word *key,* for instance, has many meanings. There are musical keys, door keys, and keys to solving a mystery. The context in which the word *key* occurs will tell you which meaning is correct.

Sometimes a word is explained by the words that immediately follow it. The subject of a sentence and your knowledge about that subject might also help you determine the meaning of an unknown word. Try to decide the meaning of the word *revive* in the following sentence:

> Sunshine and water will revive those drooping plants.

The compound subject is *sunshine* and *water.* You know that plants need light and water to survive and that drooping plants are not healthy. You can figure out that *revive* means "to bring back to health."

Distinguishing Fact from Opinion

Every day you are called upon to sort out fact and opinion. Because much of what you read and hear contains both facts and opinions, you need to be able to tell the two apart.

Facts are statements that can be proved true. The proof must be objective and verifiable. You must be able to check for yourself to confirm a fact.

Look at the following facts. Notice that they can be checked for accuracy and confirmed. Suggested sources for verification appear in parentheses.

- Abraham Lincoln was the 16th president of the United States. (Consult biographies, social studies books, encyclopedias, and similar sources.)

- Earth revolves around the Sun. (Research in encyclopedias or astronomy books; ask knowledgeable people.)

- Dogs walk on four legs. (See for yourself.)

Opinions are statements that cannot be proved true. There is no objective evidence you can consult to check the truthfulness of an opinion. Unlike facts, opinions express personal beliefs or judgments. Opinions reveal how someone feels about a subject, not the facts about that subject. You might agree or disagree with someone's opinion, but you cannot prove it right or wrong.

Look at the following opinions. The reasons these statements are classified as opinions appear in parentheses.

- Abraham Lincoln was born to be a president. (You cannot prove this by referring to birth records. There is no evidence to support this belief.)

- Earth is the only planet in our solar system where intelligent life exists. (There is no proof of this. It may be proved true some day, but for now it is just an educated guess—not a fact.)

- The dog is a human's best friend. (This is not a fact; your best friend might not be a dog.)

As you read, be aware that facts and opinions are often mixed together. Both are useful to you as a reader. But to evaluate what you read and to read intelligently, you need to know the difference between the two.

Keeping Events in Order

Sequence, or chronological order, is the order of events in a story or article or the order of steps in a process. Paying attention to the sequence of events or steps will help you follow what is happening, predict what might happen next, and make sense of a passage.

To make the sequence as clear as possible, writers often use signal words to help the reader get a more exact idea of when things happen. Following is a list of frequently used signal words and phrases:

until	first
next	then
before	after
finally	later
when	while
during	now
at the end	by the time
as soon as	in the beginning

Signal words and phrases are also useful when a writer chooses to relate details or events out of sequence. You need to pay careful attention to determine the correct chronological order.

Making Correct Inferences

Much of what you read *suggests* more than it *says*. Writers often do not state ideas directly in a text. They can't. Think of the time and space it would take to state every idea. And think of how boring that would be! Instead, writers leave it to you, the reader, to fill in the information they leave out—to make inferences. You do this by combining clues in the story or article with knowledge from your own experience.

You make many inferences every day. Suppose, for example, that you are visiting a friend's house for the first time. You see a bag of kitty litter. You infer (make an inference) that the family has a cat. Another day you overhear a conversation. You catch the names of two actors and the words *scene, dialogue,* and *directing.* You infer that the people are discussing a movie or play.

In these situations and others like them, you infer unstated information from what you observe or read. Readers must make inferences in order to understand text.

Be careful about the inferences you make. One set of facts may suggest several inferences. Some of these inferences could be faulty. A correct inference must be supported by evidence.

Remember that bag of kitty litter that caused you to infer that your friend has a cat? That could be a faulty inference. Perhaps your friend's family uses the kitty litter on their icy sidewalks to create traction. To be sure your inference is correct, you need more evidence.

Understanding Main Ideas

The main idea is the most important idea in a paragraph or passage—the idea that provides purpose and direction. The rest of the selection explains, develops, or supports the main idea. Without a main idea, there would be only a collection of unconnected thoughts.

In the following paragraph, the main idea is printed in italics. As you read, observe how the other sentences develop or explain the main idea.

Typhoon Chris hit with full fury today on the central coast of Japan. Heavy rain from the storm flooded the area. High waves carried many homes into the sea. People now fear that the heavy rains will cause mudslides in the central part of the country. The number of people killed by the storm may climb past the 200 mark by Saturday.

In this paragraph, the main-idea statement appears first. It is followed by sentences that explain, support, or give details. Sometimes the main idea appears at the end of a paragraph. Writers often put the main idea at the end of a paragraph when their purpose is to persuade or convince. Readers may be more open to a new idea if the reasons for it are presented first.

As you read the following paragraph, think about the overall impact of the supporting ideas. Their purpose is to convince the reader that the main idea in the last sentence should be accepted.

Last week there was a head-on collision at Huntington and Canton streets. Just a month ago a pedestrian was struck there. Fortunately, she was only slightly injured. In the past year, there have been more accidents there than at any other corner in the city. In fact, nearly 10 percent of all accidents in the city occur at the corner. This intersection is very dangerous, and a traffic signal should be installed there before a life is lost.

The details in the paragraph progress from least important to most important. They achieve their full effect in the main idea statement at the end.

In many cases, the main idea is not expressed in a single sentence. The reader is called upon to interpret all of the ideas expressed in the paragraph and to decide upon a main idea. Read the following paragraph.

> The American author Jack London was once a pupil at the Cole Grammar School in Oakland, California. Each morning the class sang a song. When the teacher noticed that Jack wouldn't sing, she sent him to the principal. He returned to class with a note. The note said that Jack could be excused from singing with the class if he would write an essay every morning.

In this paragraph, the reader has to interpret the individual ideas and to decide on a main idea. This main idea seems reasonable: Jack London's career as a writer began with a punishment in grammar school.

Understanding the concept of the main idea and knowing how to find it is important. Transferring that understanding to your reading and study is also important.

Working Through a Lesson

Part A

1. **Preview the article.** Locate the timed selection in Part A of the lesson that you are going to read. Wait for your teacher's signal to preview. You will have 20 seconds for previewing. Follow the previewing steps described on page 2.

2. **Read the article.** When your teacher gives you the signal, begin reading. Read carefully so that you will be able to answer questions about what you have read. When you finish reading, look at the board and note your reading time. Write this time at the bottom of the page on the line labeled Reading Time.

3. **Complete the exercises.** Answer the 10 questions that follow the article. There are 5 fact questions and 5 idea questions. Choose the best answer to each question and put an X in that box.

4. **Correct your work.** Use the Answer Key at the back of the book to check your answers. Circle any wrong answer and put an X in the box you should have marked. Record the number of correct answers on the appropriate line at the end of the lesson.

Part B

1. **Preview and read the passage.** Use the same techniques you

used to read Part A. Think about what you are reading.

2. **Complete the exercises.** Instructions are given for answering each category of question. There are 15 responses for you to record.

3. **Correct your work.** Use the Answer Key at the back of the book. Circle any wrong answer and write the correct letter or number next to it. Record the number of correct answers on the appropriate line at the end of the lesson.

Plotting Your Progress

1. **Find your reading rate.** Turn to the Reading Rate graph on page 116. Put an X at the point where the vertical line that represents the lesson intersects your reading time, shown along the left-hand side. The right-hand side of the graph will reveal your words-per-minute reading speed.

2. **Find your comprehension score.** Add your scores for Part A and Part B to determine your total number of correct answers. Turn to the Comprehension Score graph on page 117. Put an X at the point where the vertical line that represents your lesson intersects your total correct answers, shown along the left-hand side. The right-hand side of the graph will show the percentage of questions you answered correctly.

3. **Complete the Comprehension Skills Profile.** Turn to page 118. Record your incorrect answers for the Part B exercises. The five Part B skills are listed along the bottom. There are five columns of boxes, one column for each question. For every incorrect answer, put an X in a box for that skill.

To get the most benefit from these lessons, you need to take charge of your own progress in improving your reading speed and comprehension. Studying these graphs will help you to see whether your reading rate is increasing and to determine what skills you need to work on. Your teacher will also review the graphs to check your progress.

TO THE TEACHER

About the Series

Timed Readings Plus in Science includes 10 books at reading levels 4–13, with one book at each level. Book One contains material at a fourth-grade reading level; Book Two at a fifth-grade level, and so on. The readability level is determined by the Fry Readability Scale and is not to be confused with grade or age level. The books are designed for use with students at middle-school level and above.

The purposes of the series are as follows:

- to provide systematic, structured reading practice that helps students improve their reading rate and comprehension skills

- to give students practice in reading and understanding informational articles in the content area of science

- to give students experience in reading various text types—informational, expository, narrative, and prescriptive

- to prepare students for taking standardized tests that include timed reading passages in various content areas

- to provide materials with a wide range of reading levels so that students can continue to practice and improve their reading rate and comprehension skills

Because the books are designed for use with students at designated reading levels rather than in a particular grade, the science topics in this series are not correlated to any grade-level curriculum. Most standardized tests require students to read and comprehend science passages. This series provides an opportunity for students to become familiar with the particular requirements of reading science. For example, the vocabulary in a science article is important. Students need to know certain words in order to understand the concepts and the information.

Each book in the series contains 25 two-part lessons. Part A focuses on improving reading rate. This section of the lesson consists of a 400-word timed informational article on a science topic followed by two multiple-choice exercises. Recalling Facts includes five fact questions; Understanding Ideas includes five critical-thinking questions.

Part B concentrates on building mastery in critical areas of comprehension. This section consists of a nontimed passage—the "plus" passage—followed by five exercises that address five major comprehension skills. The passage varies in length; its subject matter relates to the content of the timed selection.

Timed Reading and Comprehension

Timed reading is the best-known method of improving reading speed. There is no point in someone's reading at an accelerated speed if the person does not understand what she or he is reading. Nothing is more important than comprehension in reading. The main purpose of reading is to gain knowledge and insight, to understand the information that the writer and the text are communicating.

Few students will be able to read a passage once and answer all of the questions correctly. A score of 70 to 80 percent correct is normal. If the student gets 90 to 100 percent correct, he or she is either reading too slowly or the material is at too low a reading level. A comprehension or critical thinking score of less than 70 percent indicates a need for improvement.

One method of improving comprehension and critical-thinking skills is for the student to go back and study each incorrect answer. First, the student should reread the question carefully. It is surprising how many students get the wrong answer simply because they have not read the question carefully. Then the student should look back in the passage to find the place where the question is answered, reread that part of the passage, and think about how to arrive at the correct answer. It is important to be able to recognize a correct answer when it is embedded in the text. Teacher guidance or class discussion will help the student find an answer.

Speed Versus Comprehension

It is not unusual for comprehension scores to decline as reading rate increases during the early weeks of timed readings. If this happens, students should attempt to level off their speed—but not lower it—and concentrate more on comprehension. Usually, if students maintain the higher speed and concentrate on comprehension, scores will gradually improve and within a week or two be back up to normal levels of 70 to 80 percent.

It is important to achieve a proper balance between speed and comprehension. An inefficient reader typically reads everything at one speed, usually slowly. Some poor readers, however, read rapidly but without satisfactory comprehension. It is important to achieve a balance between speed and comprehension. The practice that this series provides enables students to increase their reading speed while maintaining normal levels of comprehension.

Getting Started

As a rule, the passages in a book designed to improve reading speed should be relatively easy. The student should not have much difficulty with the vocabulary or the subject matter. Don't worry about the passages being too easy; students should see how quickly and efficiently they can read a passage.

Begin by assigning students to a level. A student should start with a book that is one level below his or her current reading level. If a student's reading level is not known, a suitable starting point would be one or two levels below the student's present grade in school.

Introduce students to the contents and format of the book they are using. Examine the book to see how it is organized. Talk about the parts of each lesson. Discuss the purpose of timed reading and the use of the progress graphs at the back of the book.

Timing the Reading

One suggestion for timing the reading is to have all students begin reading the selection at the same time. After one minute, write on the board the time that has elapsed and begin updating it at 10-second intervals (1:00, 1:10, 1:20, etc.). Another option is to have individual students time themselves with a stopwatch.

Teaching a Lesson

Part A

1. Give students the signal to begin previewing the lesson. Allow 20 seconds, then discuss special science terms or vocabulary that students found.

2. Use one of the methods described above to time students as they read the passage. (Include the 20-second preview time as part of the first minute.) Tell students to write down the last time shown on the board or the stopwatch when they finish reading. Have them record the time in the designated space after the passage.

3. Next, have students complete the exercises in Part A. Work with them to check their answers, using the Answer Key that begins on page 114. Have them circle incorrect answers, mark the correct answers, and then record the numbers of correct answers for Part A on the appropriate line at the end of the lesson. Correct responses to eight or more questions indicate satisfactory comprehension and recall.

Part B

1. Have students read the Part B passage and complete the exercises that follow it. Directions are provided with each exercise. Correct responses require deliberation and discrimination.

2. Work with students to check their answers. Then discuss the answers with them and have them record the number of correct answers for Part B at the end of the lesson.

Have students study the correct answers to the questions they answered incorrectly. It is important that they understand why a particular answer is correct or incorrect.

Have them reread relevant parts of a passage to clarify an answer. An effective cooperative activity is to have students work in pairs to discuss their answers, explain why they chose the answers they did, and try to resolve differences.

Monitoring Progress

Have students find their total correct answers for the lesson and record their reading time and scores on the graphs on pages 116 and 117. Then have them complete the Comprehension Skills Profile on page 118. For each incorrect response to a question in Part B, students should mark an X in the box above each question type.

The legend on the Reading Rate graph automatically converts reading times to words-per-minute rates. The Comprehension Score graph automatically converts the raw scores to percentages.

These graphs provide a visual record of a student's progress. This record gives the student and you an opportunity to evaluate the student's progress and to determine the types of exercises and skills he or she needs to concentrate on.

Diagnosis and Evaluation

The following are typical reading rates.

Slow Reader—150 Words Per Minute

Average Reader—250 Words Per Minute

Fast Reader—350 Words Per Minute

A student who consistently reads at an average or above-average rate (with satisfactory comprehension) is ready to advance to the next book in the series.

A column of Xs in the Comprehension Skills Profile indicates a specific comprehension weakness. Using the profile, you can assess trends in student performance and suggest remedial work if necessary.

For centuries people dreamed of space travel. This dream began to seem possible with the development of high-flying rockets in the early 1900s. A rocket travels through the air by shooting out a stream of hot gases. These gases come from the burning of fuel.

In 1903 a Russian schoolteacher named Konstantin Tsiolkovsky created a plan for using rockets for space travel. His plan was the first one to include accurate scientific calculations. About 20 years later, a U.S. scientist named Robert Goddard built the first rockets that could reach high altitudes. In Germany in the 1920s, Hermann Oberth wrote a book that persuaded many powerful people that the new rockets made space flight possible. During World War II, German scientists designed large rockets that could travel long distances while carrying high explosives. After the war, scientists from Germany went to the United States and the Soviet Union to help design space rockets.

Those two countries were soon in a race to space. The competition was intense because of their competing political systems and military might. The Soviet Union had a communist system, and the United States has a democratic one. The two rivals also had developed hydrogen bombs. People in the United States became concerned when the Soviets were the first to launch a space satellite, which was called *Sputnik*. The Soviets were also first in sending a person into space when Yury Gagarin traveled in the *Vostok 1* spacecraft in 1961.

The U.S. government became determined that its space program would be the first to put a person on the Moon. The U.S. space program built a series of *Apollo* spacecraft, which were powered by huge Saturn 5 rockets. In 1969, *Apollo 11* took three men to the Moon. Neil Armstrong became the first person to set foot on the Moon.

After the Soviets lost the race to land people on the Moon, they built the first space station. The United States also built a space station. The space stations proved that people could live and work in space. The Soviet Union and the United States linked two spacecraft in space on a joint mission. This ended their "space race." Today a much larger space station, assembled with the cooperation of several countries, orbits Earth.

Another first in space travel was the space shuttle, which looks like an airplane. Astronauts on the shuttle have launched satellites, helped construct space stations, and conducted scientific experiments.

Reading Time _____

Recalling Facts

1. The first person to build high-altitude rockets was
   - ❑ a. Neil Armstrong.
   - ❑ b. Hermann Oberth.
   - ❑ c. Robert Goddard.

2. The two countries that were in a space race were
   - ❑ a. the Soviet Union and the United States.
   - ❑ b. Germany and the United States.
   - ❑ c. the Soviet Union and Germany.

3. The first person to travel in space was
   - ❑ a. Neil Armstrong.
   - ❑ b. Yury Gagarin.
   - ❑ c. Hermann Oberth.

4. The spacecraft that carried the first person to land on the Moon was
   - ❑ a. *Apollo 11.*
   - ❑ b. *Vostok 1.*
   - ❑ c. *Sputnik.*

5. The space station that is currently orbiting Earth was built by
   - ❑ a. several countries.
   - ❑ b. only the United States and the Soviet Union.
   - ❑ c. Japan and Germany.

Understanding Ideas

6. One can conclude from reading this article that space travel would not be possible without the invention of
   - ❑ a. rockets.
   - ❑ b. the space shuttle.
   - ❑ c. Skylab.

7. Americans most likely were concerned by *Sputnik* because
   - ❑ a. it appeared that the Soviets had better scientists.
   - ❑ b. they were worried that *Sputnik* contained bombs.
   - ❑ c. there were no U.S. rockets.

8. One could conclude that the technology developed by the U.S. space program has
   - ❑ a. become entirely out of date.
   - ❑ b. been a total waste of money.
   - ❑ c. led to the development of valuable satellites.

9. People's living and working in space was thought to be an important development probably because
   - ❑ a. scientists were not sure how long people could survive in space.
   - ❑ b. it marked the end of space exploration.
   - ❑ c. photographs of planets were available for the first time.

10. This article suggests that
    - ❑ a. the space race was won by the United States.
    - ❑ b. the space race was won by the Soviet Union.
    - ❑ c. both the United States and the Soviet Union made the dream of space travel come true.

Neil Armstrong: First Person on the Moon

Neil Armstrong was born in Ohio in 1930. As a young boy, he made model airplanes. He got his pilot's license at age 16. He went to college and then became a pilot in the U.S. Navy. He was awarded medals for combat missions he flew during the Korean War. Later, he was a test pilot who flew newly designed jet aircraft. Then he became an astronaut.

Armstrong commanded the *Gemini 8* space mission in 1966 and helped get the spacecraft out of a precarious situation. In 1969 Armstrong, Buzz Aldrin, and Michael Collins flew to the Moon on the *Apollo 11* spacecraft. First the spacecraft went into orbit around the Moon. Then Armstrong and Aldrin flew the small lunar module, the *Eagle,* to the Moon's surface. After a safe landing, Armstrong said, "The *Eagle* has landed." People on Earth could hardly believe that astronauts were actually on the Moon!

Armstrong was the first to set foot on the Moon. He said, "That's one small step for man; one giant leap for mankind." Armstrong and Aldrin explored the Moon's surface. They took photos and picked up Moon rocks and dust. They set up equipment to record data about the Moon. They left behind a U.S. flag and their footprints. Because there is no air or wind on the Moon, the footprints may stay there for millions of years.

1. Recognizing Words in Context

Find the word *precarious* in the passage. One definition below is closest to the meaning of that word. One definition has the opposite or nearly opposite meaning. The remaining definition has a completely different meaning. Label the definitions C for *closest,* O for *opposite or nearly opposite,* and D for *different.*

_____ a. planned

_____ b. safe

_____ c. dangerous

2. Distinguishing Fact from Opinion

Two of the statements below present *facts,* which can be proved correct. The other statement is an *opinion,* which expresses someone's thoughts or beliefs. Label the statements F for *fact* and O for *opinion.*

_____ a. Neil Armstrong was born in Ohio in 1930.

_____ b. Armstrong showed a tremendous amount of courage as an astronaut.

_____ c. The *Apollo 11* mission included a Moon landing.

3. **Keeping Events in Order**

Label the statements below 1, 2, and 3 to show the order in which the events happened.

_____ a. *Apollo 11* began orbiting the Moon.

_____ b. The *Eagle* landed safely on the Moon.

_____ c. Armstrong and Aldrin began flying the *Eagle*.

4. **Making Correct Inferences**

Two of the statements below are correct *inferences,* or reasonable guesses. They are based on information in the passage. The other statement is an incorrect, or faulty, inference. Label the statements C for *correct* inference and F for *faulty* inference.

_____ a. Astronauts have dangerous jobs.

_____ b. Moon rocks can provide valuable information about the Moon's history.

_____ c. Scientists now know everything there is to know about the Moon.

5. **Understanding Main Ideas**

One of the statements below expresses the main idea of the passage. One statement is too general, or too broad. The other explains only part of the passage; it is too narrow. Label the statements M for *main idea*, B for *too broad,* and N for *too narrow.*

_____ a. Neil Armstrong is famous for being the first person on the Moon.

_____ b. Astronauts have accomplished some amazing things.

_____ c. Neil Armstrong collected Moon rocks and dust.

Correct Answers, Part A _____

Correct Answers, Part B _____

Total Correct Answers _____

What Is a Botanist?

Botany is the science of plants. A plant is a living thing that is unable to move around by itself and has no nervous system. A botanist is a scientist who studies plants.

Some botanists identify and classify plants. Their work is called plant taxonomy. Botanists organize plants into groups according to the plants' structures. There are two main groups, or phyla, of plants. One phylum is made up of plants that are more complex than other plants. These are called vascular plants. They have tissues that move water and food through the plant. Some examples are trees, herbs, and shrubs.

The second phylum is made up of simpler plants that do not have true roots, stems, or leaves. They are called nonvascular plants because they do not have special tissues for moving water and food. Two examples are moss and liverworts. The two plant phyla are divided into many smaller groups according to the way some plants are similar to others.

Early botanists learned about the nature of plants through research. They learned how green plants make their own food, how plant cells work, and how plants reproduce. In the 1600s a British scientist named Robert Hooke used one of the first microscopes to learn that plants have cells. Later, it was found that all living things have cells. An Austrian monk named Gregor Mendel, who lived in the 1800s, studied how plants inherit characteristics. He bred pea plants that varied in appearance and carefully recorded what each generation of plants looked like.

Some botanists study plant fossils to learn about Earth's ancient history. A fossil is a trace or an imprint left in rock by a dead plant or animal. Plants appeared on Earth before animals did, so the oldest fossils are those of plants. Knowing what kinds of plants lived in an area can tell scientists what the environment was like. If scientists find fossils of ocean plants in an area that is now a desert, they know there was once an ocean there.

Botanists do many other kinds of work. Some teach at schools. Some study how plants can be used to make medicines. Others work to produce new types of crops. A botanist might develop a strain of corn that insects do not find tasty. Botanists work in forest management and help to breed new trees. In ecology, botanists study how plants are affected by their environment.

Reading Time _____

Recalling Facts

1. All plants are living things that
   - ❏ a. have tissue that moves food.
   - ❏ b. are unable to move around by themselves.
   - ❏ c. leave fossils in layers of rock.

2. The science of classifying plants is called
   - ❏ a. taxonomy.
   - ❏ b. heredity.
   - ❏ c. ecology.

3. Botanists organize plants into groups according to the plants'
   - ❏ a. color.
   - ❏ b. height.
   - ❏ c. structure.

4. The oldest fossils are those of
   - ❏ a. plants.
   - ❏ b. humans.
   - ❏ c. dinosaurs.

5. Robert Hooke discovered that plants had
   - ❏ a. tissue.
   - ❏ b. seeds.
   - ❏ c. cells.

Understanding Ideas

6. Which topic would a botanist be least likely to study?
   - ❏ a. the age of fossils
   - ❏ b. the properties of electricity
   - ❏ c. the breeding of fruit trees

7. An apple tree is a
   - ❏ a. vascular plant.
   - ❏ b. nonvascular plant.
   - ❏ c. simple plant.

8. Which plants belong to the same phylum?
   - ❏ a. a rose bush and a moss
   - ❏ b. a rose bush and a liverwort
   - ❏ c. a rose bush and a pine tree

9. You can infer from the article that the relationship between the words *phylum* and *phyla* is that
   - ❏ a. *phylum* is plural, and *phyla* is singular.
   - ❏ b. *phylum* is singular, and *phyla* is plural.
   - ❏ c. *phyla* is used only with nonvascular plants.

10. The most likely place to find a plant fossil is
    - ❏ a. on a sandy beach.
    - ❏ b. on the bark of a tree.
    - ❏ c. along the banks of a rocky stream.

Do Plants Feel Pain?

When plants are injured, they respond in particular ways. Does this mean that plants feel pain the way humans do?

Humans and animals have nervous systems and, usually, brains as well. When an animal is hurt, nerve endings sense the damage and send that information to the brain. The brain registers the pain and directs the body to respond in certain ways. Unlike animals, plants do not have brains or nerves. Therefore, they do not feel pain, at least the type of pain that humans and animals experience.

The ability to feel pain would not benefit plants the way it benefits animals. In animals, pain serves as a warning. They respond by moving away from whatever is causing the pain. Because plants cannot move, they have no use for this kind of warning system.

Although plants do not feel pain, they do respond to injury. When injured, plants speed up some of their chemical processes. They take in more carbon dioxide gas from the air. They use this gas to change stored food into materials that they can use to make new cells to heal the injury. They also increase their production of phenols, which are chemicals that protect against cell damage. If an injury is severe, however, it may disrupt the basic processes of the plant and kill the plant.

1. **Recognizing Words in Context**

   Find the word *disrupt* in the passage. One definition below is closest to the meaning of that word. One definition has the opposite or nearly opposite meaning. The remaining definition has a completely different meaning. Label the definitions C for *closest*, O for *opposite or nearly opposite*, and D for *different*.

   _____ a. break up

   _____ b. fix

   _____ c. criticize

2. **Distinguishing Fact from Opinion**

   Two of the statements below present *facts*, which can be proved correct. The other statement is an *opinion*, which expresses someone's thoughts or beliefs. Label the statements F for *fact* and O for *opinion*.

   _____ a. Plants do not have nervous systems.

   _____ b. People who damage plants should have a good reason for doing so.

   _____ c. A plant can grow new cells to help heal an injury.

3. **Keeping Events in Order**

Label the statements below 1, 2, and 3 to show the order in which the events happen.

_____ a. A deer eats some bark off a young tree.

_____ b. A young tree begins to take in more carbon dioxide.

_____ c. A young tree produces new cells to replace some of the bark.

4. **Making Correct Inferences**

Two of the statements below are correct *inferences,* or reasonable guesses. They are based on information in the passage. The other statement is an incorrect, or faulty, inference. Label the statements C for *correct* inference and F for *faulty* inference.

_____ a. The injured part of a plant sends chemical signals to the rest of the plant.

_____ b. Plants do not have feelings of any kind.

_____ c. Plant cells are completely different from animal cells.

5. **Understanding Main Ideas**

One of the statements below expresses the main idea of the passage. One statement is too general, or too broad. The other explains only part of the passage; it is too narrow. Label the statements M for *main idea,* B for *too broad,* and N for *too narrow.*

_____ a. Plants respond when they are injured but do not feel pain as humans do.

_____ b. Plants can't move away from danger.

_____ c. Plants are living things.

Correct Answers, Part A _____

Correct Answers, Part B _____

Total Correct Answers _____

Earth has several kinds of bodies of water. Two of the most important are lakes and rivers, because they are vital to the well-being of humans and animals. Lakes and rivers are the source of 70 percent of the drinking water in the United States. They also provide homes for many species of animals and plants.

A lake is a large body of water that does not flow anywhere and is not directly connected to an ocean. Lakes are entirely or almost entirely surrounded by land. Some lakes were formed after large masses of ice called glaciers moved over the land, carving out rock and soil. These lakes are called glacial lakes. The Great Lakes are glacial lakes. Some lakes were formed when landslides blocked valleys. These are called barrier lakes. When rain and melted snow collect in the craters of volcanoes, they form crater lakes, such as Crater Lake in Oregon. Tectonic lakes form in cracks in Earth's crust. These cracks are formed by the underground movements of large masses of rock called plates. Lake Tanganyika in East Africa is a tectonic lake.

A river is a large body of water that flows down a slope to an ocean or a lake. A river starts at a source, which can be a spring, a lake, or melted snow that has run off a mountain. The place where a river ends is called its mouth. This is where the river runs into the ocean or lake. A river can grow in size as it moves from its source to its mouth. It may be joined along the way by smaller rivers and streams. These are called tributaries.

The source of the Mississippi River is a lake in Minnesota. The river starts as a stream so small a person can step across it. It flows south and widens as rivers and streams join it. It flows for about 2,000 miles (3,200 kilometers) to its mouth in the Gulf of Mexico.

A river and its tributaries make up a river system. The entire region that supplies water to a river is called a drainage basin. One drainage basin is separated from another by a line of high land called a watershed, or divide.

Rivers provide water for growing crops. They can be used to transport goods by boat. River water also can generate electricity by means of hydroelectric dams.

Reading Time _____

Recalling Facts

1. A lake
   - ❑ a. flows down a slope.
   - ❑ b. has a source and a mouth.
   - ❑ c. sits in a low area and is surrounded by land.

2. A barrier lake is formed in a
   - ❑ a. crater of a dead volcano.
   - ❑ b. valley blocked by a landslide.
   - ❑ c. crack in Earth's crust.

3. A river is a body of water that
   - ❑ a. flows down a slope and into an ocean or a lake.
   - ❑ b. is always a result of melting snow.
   - ❑ c. flows for more than 1,000 kilometers.

4. Rivers and streams that flow into a river are called
   - ❑ a. springs.
   - ❑ b. currents.
   - ❑ c. tributaries.

5. Lakes and rivers are the source of _____ percent of the drinking water in the United States.
   - ❑ a. 25
   - ❑ b. 40
   - ❑ c. 70

Understanding Ideas

6. One can infer from the article that lakes are
   - ❑ a. sometimes formed by the movement of rock or ice.
   - ❑ b. wide sections of rivers.
   - ❑ c. always very deep.

7. A tectonic lake would be most likely to result from
   - ❑ a. a thunderstorm.
   - ❑ b. an earthquake.
   - ❑ c. a watershed.

8. A river is most likely to be widest at
   - ❑ a. its source.
   - ❑ b. a point where it is joined by a stream.
   - ❑ c. its mouth.

9. Without lakes and rivers,
   - ❑ a. most animals would die.
   - ❑ b. the oceans would dry up.
   - ❑ c. there would be no mountains or valleys.

10. Which of the following would you be most likely to find in a river's drainage basin?
    - ❑ a. a sand dune
    - ❑ b. a volcano
    - ❑ c. a marsh

Cleaning Up Rivers

Many people believe that river pollution is a big problem. Part of the water that supplies rivers comes from rain that seeps through the ground. This water, called groundwater, may combine with pesticides and other chemicals as it moves through the soil. The chemicals can kill fish and make river water unsafe to drink.

Pollution becomes worse when rivers can't flow freely. Groundwater can carry fertilizer from farmland into rivers. The fertilizer can make river plants grow faster and clog the river. As river water backs up, it can become more concentrated with pollutants. Trash dumped into rivers is another source of pollution.

Toxic wastes pollute many of Earth's rivers. Factories sometimes dump these wastes into rivers because it is an inexpensive way to get rid of pollutants. People sometimes pour wastes such as motor oil and paint down drains. These wastes are difficult to remove from water and can find their way into rivers.

In 1972 Congress passed the Clean Water Act. Since that time, industry has had to meet pollution standards for wastewater. The law also protects wetlands. Because of this law, rivers are cleaner. But pollution is still a problem in some areas. Some environmental groups check to make sure that factories obey clean-water laws. Volunteer groups clear trash from rivers so that the water can flow freely. Cities have waste collection days. People bring in old oil, paint, and chemicals instead of pouring them down the drain.

1. **Recognizing Words in Context**

   Find the word *toxic* in the passage. One definition below is closest to the meaning of that word. One definition has the opposite or nearly opposite meaning. The remaining definition has a completely different meaning. Label the definitions C for *closest,* O for *opposite or nearly opposite,* and D for *different.*

   _____ a. wet

   _____ b. poisonous

   _____ c. safe

2. **Distinguishing Fact from Opinion**

   Two of the statements below present *facts,* which can be proved correct. The other statement is an *opinion,* which expresses someone's thoughts or beliefs. Label the statements F for *fact* and O for *opinion.*

   _____ a. Some groups are working to reduce river pollution.

   _____ b. Polluted groundwater is one of our country's most serious problems.

   _____ c. Pesticides and other chemicals can kill fish.

3. Keeping Events in Order

Label the statements below 1, 2, and 3 to show the order in which the events happen.

_____ a. Rain is absorbed into the soil, where it combines with pesticides.

_____ b. A heavy rain falls on a field of corn.

_____ c. Polluted groundwater flows into a river.

4. Making Correct Inferences

Two of the statements below are correct *inferences,* or reasonable guesses. They are based on information in the passage. The other statement is an incorrect, or faulty, inference. Label the statements C for *correct* inference and F for *faulty* inference.

_____ a. Pesticides cause rivers to flow more slowly.

_____ b. The Clean Water Act was passed because pollution had gotten worse and worse.

_____ c. The businesses that pollute the most are trying to make as much money as possible.

5. Understanding Main Ideas

One of the statements below expresses the main idea of the passage. One statement is too general, or too broad. The other explains only part of the passage; it is too narrow. Label the statements M for *main idea,* B for *too broad,* and N for *too narrow.*

_____ a. The Clean Water Act was passed in 1972.

_____ b. River pollution has decreased, but it is still a problem.

_____ c. Pollution has many bad effects.

Correct Answers, Part A _____

Correct Answers, Part B _____

Total Correct Answers _____

How Flight Is Possible

A jet plane moves down an airport runway, picking up speed until it lifts off the ground. A bird flaps its wings and takes off into the sky. Once in flight, both the plane and the bird soar smoothly through the air. What makes each one able to take off and remain in the air?

The answer lies partly in their body structures. The body of a bird is covered with feathers, and it is lightweight because many of the bones are hollow. The shape of its wings and tapered body are ideal for flight. Like birds, airplanes have tapered bodies with wings. Unlike birds, planes have engines that allow them to lift off and remain in flight. Flight is possible for both birds and planes because they are able to deal with four forces involved in flight. These forces are lift, thrust, drag, and gravity.

Lift is produced as the wings of a bird or a plane move through air. Both kinds of wings are curved on top and flat on the bottom. Air flows more quickly over the curved top than it does over the flat bottom. This reduces the air pressure above the wing, which pulls the bird or plane upward.

Thrust is needed to make air flow over the wings to achieve lift. Thrust is the force that propels a bird or plane forward. To create thrust, a bird flaps its wings, and a plane uses one or more engines.

Drag is caused by air flowing against the body of the plane or the bird. Drag is a force that pushes against an object and slows it down. The tapered body of birds and planes gives them a streamlined quality and helps reduce drag so that they can gather enough speed to lift off.

Gravity is the force that both planes and birds must overcome to get off the ground. A plane is heavy and needs a lot of thrust to produce enough lift to overcome gravity and take off. In the air, the shape of the bird or plane creates balance so that gravity does not cause it to nose-dive or pitch to the side. The tails of birds and planes are important in maintaining balance. Birds and planes are able to adjust their directions by moving their wings and tails slightly. They also must make adjustments to deal with changes in wind speed and direction.

Reading Time _____

Recalling Facts

1. Birds' bodies are lightweight partly because they have many
   - ❑ a. small organs.
   - ❑ b. hollow bones.
   - ❑ c. feathery wings.

2. Lift, thrust, drag, and gravity are
   - ❑ a. forces involved in flight.
   - ❑ b. built into modern-day jets.
   - ❑ c. types of air pressure.

3. A force that pulls birds and planes upward as air flows past wings is
   - ❑ a. gravity.
   - ❑ b. magnetism.
   - ❑ c. lift.

4. The flapping wings of a bird and the engine of a plane both produce
   - ❑ a. thrust.
   - ❑ b. drag.
   - ❑ c. gravity.

5. The wings of birds and planes are _____ on top.
   - ❑ a. flat
   - ❑ b. curved
   - ❑ c. tapered

Understanding Ideas

6. You can infer that "tapered body" means a body that is
   - ❑ a. smaller at the back than at the front.
   - ❑ b. full of energy.
   - ❑ c. connected to wings and feet.

7. You can conclude from the article that without a tail, a bird or plane would have trouble
   - ❑ a. overcoming gravity.
   - ❑ b. taking off.
   - ❑ c. changing directions.

8. Although a bird needs only to flap its wings to fly, a plane needs an engine to provide thrust because
   - ❑ a. it is not lightweight.
   - ❑ b. it has long wings.
   - ❑ c. it has narrow wings.

9. You can infer that the largest airplanes need to have
   - ❑ a. very thick wings.
   - ❑ b. as few passengers as possible.
   - ❑ c. very powerful engines.

10. The article suggests that flight is possible mainly because of
    - ❑ a. body structure alone.
    - ❑ b. thrust and body structure.
    - ❑ c. powerful wings and jet engines.

4 B   Helicopters: Form and Function

Like an airplane, a helicopter is a machine that can fly. But the body of a helicopter is not much like the body of a plane. Instead of wings, a helicopter has rotors, which look like giant propellers. Most helicopters have one large rotor on top and a smaller rotor on the tail. As the engine spins the blades of the large rotor, air is pushed down, and the craft is pulled up. The rotor can be tilted slightly to make the helicopter go in a specific direction. The rotor on the tail also is used to control direction.

The rotors allow the helicopter to move in special ways. Unlike planes, which must move forward to stay in flight, helicopters can hover in one spot for a long time. They can also move straight up and down. When landing, they do not need a runway. They can land on any small, flat space, even one that is on top of a building.

Helicopters are used in many kinds of rescue work because they can hover and make precise movements. The police and coast guard use them to search for missing people. If someone is seriously injured in a remote area that cannot be reached by ambulance, a helicopter can take the person to a hospital.

1. **Recognizing Words in Context**

   Find the word *hover* in the passage. One definition below is closest to the meaning of that word. One definition has the opposite or nearly opposite meaning. The remaining definition has a completely different meaning. Label the definitions C for *closest*, O for *opposite or nearly opposite*, and D for *different*.

   _____ a. move in circles

   _____ b. float in the same place

   _____ c. move away quickly

2. **Distinguishing Fact from Opinion**

   Two of the statements below present *facts*, which can be proved correct. The other statement is an *opinion*, which expresses someone's thoughts or beliefs. Label the statements F for *fact* and O for *opinion*.

   _____ a. Rotors allow a helicopter to move in special ways.

   _____ b. Helicopters are used in rescue missions.

   _____ c. Helicopters are more valuable than jets.

3. Keeping Events in Order

Label the statements below 1, 2, and 3 to show the order in which the events happen.

_____ a. The rotor starts to turn.

_____ b. The helicopter rises off the ground.

_____ c. Air is pushed down by a strong force.

4. Making Correct Inferences

Two of the statements below are correct *inferences*, or reasonable guesses. They are based on information in the passage. The other statement is an incorrect, or faulty, inference. Label the statements C for *correct* inference and F for *faulty* inference.

_____ a. It is dangerous for helicopters to land near trees.

_____ b. Helicopters can land on top of a hill.

_____ c. Helicopter rescues are always successful.

5. Understanding Main Ideas

One of the statements below expresses the main idea of the passage. One statement is too general, or too broad. The other explains only part of the passage; it is too narrow. Label the statements M for *main idea*, B for *too broad*, and N for *too narrow*.

_____ a. Aircraft can be used for many different purposes.

_____ b. Helicopters can be used to transport people to hospitals.

_____ c. The structure of a helicopter allows it to move in special ways and to perform unique tasks.

Correct Answers, Part A _____

Correct Answers, Part B _____

Total Correct Answers _____

The planet Earth is made of four layers: the crust, the mantle, the outer core, and the inner core. Earth is changing all the time because of the high pressures and temperatures deep inside it.

The surface, or crust, of Earth is made up of rocky sections, called plates, that move very slowly. Land is made of continental crust, which is mainly granite. Most of this crust formed when hot, liquid rock called magma rose from below and hardened. Beneath the oceans lies the oceanic crust, which is made up primarily of the minerals silicon oxide and magnesium oxide. These minerals come mainly from volcanoes. Earth's crust has an average thickness of about 10 kilometers (6 miles) under the oceans. Under the continents the average thickness is about 40 kilometers (23 miles). The crust is a thin layer in comparison to the layers below it.

Unlike the crust, which is hard and thin, the mantle is soft and thick. It is made of very hot rock that flows like hot asphalt. Substances that contain iron make up most of this hot rock. The mantle is about 2,900 kilometers (1,800 miles) thick and is Earth's thickest layer. The lower part of the mantle is hotter than the upper part. It is thought that the hottest material at the bottom rises and then sinks as it cools. The movements of liquid rock in the mantle cause movements in the crust above.

The mantle surrounds Earth's outer core. In contrast to the mantle, the outer core is so much hotter that the metals found there are liquid. They consist mainly of iron and nickel. The outer core is about 2,300 kilometers (1,400 miles) thick. Beneath it lies the inner core, which is the center of Earth. This globe-shaped area has a radius of about 1,300 kilometers (800 miles). It is the hottest and heaviest layer of all. Like the outer core, it is made up mainly of iron and nickel. Unlike the metal in the outer core, the metal in the inner core is solid because of the tremendous amount of pressure there.

Scientists believe that when Earth was a young planet, it collided with many other objects during the formation of the solar system. This made Earth very hot. As it cooled, the heaviest material sank to the center and remained hot. The lightest material moved out to form the crust.

Reading Time _____

Recalling Facts

1. The oceanic crust
   - ❑ a. lies only under the ocean.
   - ❑ b. is part of Earth's mantle.
   - ❑ c. lies under both the ocean and the continents.

2. Earth's crust is
   - ❑ a. hard and thin.
   - ❑ b. soft and thick.
   - ❑ c. soft and thin.

3. The mantle is made of
   - ❑ a. very hot rock that flows like hot asphalt.
   - ❑ b. liquid metals.
   - ❑ c. solid metals.

4. Earth's thickest layer is
   - ❑ a. the crust.
   - ❑ b. the mantle.
   - ❑ c. the outer core.

5. As the young Earth cooled, the heaviest material
   - ❑ a. sank to the center.
   - ❑ b. rose to the top.
   - ❑ c. formed the mantle.

Understanding Ideas

6. One can best show Earth's layers by using a
   - ❑ a. round rock.
   - ❑ b. peach half, showing the skin, flesh, and pit.
   - ❑ c. a slice of frosted cake.

7. From the information about Earth's layers given in this article, one can conclude that
   - ❑ a. the deeper the layer, the hotter the temperature.
   - ❑ b. the deeper the layer, the cooler the temperature.
   - ❑ c. each layer is about the same temperature.

8. It is most likely that the high pressure in the inner core comes from
   - ❑ a. the weight of the layers above the inner core.
   - ❑ b. gases deep inside Earth.
   - ❑ c. high temperatures.

9. From the information in the article, you can conclude that
   - ❑ a. iron will melt only at a very high temperature.
   - ❑ b. Earth is made entirely of pure iron and substances that contain iron.
   - ❑ c. all layers of Earth are divided into plates.

10. You can infer that earthquakes are caused by
    - ❑ a. the movements of plates.
    - ❑ b. large ocean waves.
    - ❑ c. the solid iron in the inner core.

5　　B　　Making a Model of Earth's Layers

A model of Earth's layers can be made by using some common materials. This is a project for two students to do together. An adult should supervise. The materials needed are wax paper, wire, brown paint, a paintbrush, three small stick-on labels, and red, orange, yellow, and blue modeling clay.

Step One: Spread the wax paper over a table or work surface.

Step Two: Roll some red modeling clay into a ball about the size of a small marble. This represents the hottest layer of Earth, its inner core. Cover the red clay with a layer of orange clay until the ball is the size of a large marble. The orange represents the outer core.

Step Three: Use yellow clay to cover the orange ball. Keep adding yellow clay until the ball is a little bigger than a golf ball. The yellow clay signifies Earth's mantle, the thickest layer.

Step Four: Cover the yellow ball with a thin layer of blue clay. This represents Earth's crust, which is thin and cool.

Step Five: Use the wire to slice the ball carefully in half. Each person should take one half of "Earth."

Step Six: Use brown paint to draw continents on half of the ball. Allow the paint to dry.

Step Seven: Write *core, mantle,* and *crust* on three stick-on labels. Use them to label the layers of "Earth."

1. **Recognizing Words in Context**

   Find the word *signifies* in the passage. One definition below is closest to the meaning of that word. One definition has the opposite or nearly opposite meaning. The remaining definition has a completely different meaning. Label the definitions C for *closest,* O for *opposite or nearly opposite,* and D for *different.*

   _____ a. represents

   _____ b. surrounds

   _____ c. contradicts

2. **Distinguishing Fact from Opinion**

   Two of the statements below present *facts,* which can be proved correct. The other statement is an *opinion,* which expresses someone's thoughts or beliefs. Label the statements F for *fact* and O for *opinion.*

   _____ a. The hottest layer of Earth is its inner core.

   _____ b. Earth's crust is made up of plates.

   _____ c. Making a model is the best way to learn about the structure of something.

3. **Keeping Events in Order**

Label the statements below 1, 2, and 3 to show the order in which the steps should be performed.

_____ a. Use orange clay to cover the red clay.

_____ b. Roll some red clay into a ball the size of a small marble.

_____ c. Cover the orange ball with a layer of yellow clay.

4. **Making Correct Inferences**

Two of the statements below are correct *inferences*, or reasonable guesses. They are based on information in the passage. The other statement is an incorrect, or faulty, inference. Label the statements C for *correct* inference and F for *faulty* inference.

_____ a. A model of Earth's layers can show the difference in the thicknesses of the layers.

_____ b. The different colors of the clay represent the different temperatures of the layers.

_____ c. An egg provides another good model of Earth's layers.

5. **Understanding Main Ideas**

One of the statements below expresses the main idea of the passage. One statement is too general, or too broad. The other explains only part of the passage; it is too narrow. Label the statements M for *main idea*, B for *too broad*, and N for *too narrow*.

_____ a. Blue clay can be used to represent Earth's crust.

_____ b. Models can be used to explain important science concepts.

_____ c. Different colored modeling clays can be used to make a model of Earth's layers.

Correct Answers, Part A _____

Correct Answers, Part B _____

Total Correct Answers _____

The Nobel Prizes

The Nobel Prizes are named for Alfred Nobel. Nobel was a Swedish chemist who invented dynamite. He invented many other things as well, and he built companies around the world. He became very rich. He also wrote poetry and worked for world peace.

Alfred Nobel died in 1895. In his will, he left about $9 million to establish a fund to award prizes. The prizes were to be given out once a year to persons who had best helped humanity.

The will indicated that there were to be prizes in five categories. One prize would be for the most important discovery in physics. Physics is the science that studies the relationship between objects and energy. Another prize would be for chemistry. This is the study of substances and their properties. The third prize would be for important work in medicine. A fourth prize would be for literature. The fifth prize would go to a person who worked for world peace. Nobel instructed that the judges who selected the winners were not to take into consideration where a person lived.

The first Nobel Prizes were awarded in 1901. In addition to money, each prize includes a medal and a diploma. The diploma is a document that honors the person who has earned the prize. In 1969 the Bank of Sweden provided money to add a prize in economics. Economics is the study of the buying and selling of goods and services.

At first, more than three people could share one Nobel Prize. This rule was changed; now no more than three people can share a prize, unless all of them belong to the same organization working for peace. Sometimes two people win a prize. Other times just one person does. There have been years when no prize has been awarded in particular categories. Since 1950 only the Nobel Prize in peace has not been awarded every year.

Perhaps the most famous scientist to win a Nobel Prize was Albert Einstein. He was awarded the Nobel Prize in physics in 1921. Einstein received his award for his brilliance in combining physics with mathematics and his studies of the properties of light. Some scientists have won more than one Nobel Prize. Linus Pauling won Nobel Prizes in both chemistry and peace. Marie Curie won prizes in both physics and chemistry. A Nobel Prize is considered one of the world's greatest honors.

Reading Time _____

Recalling Facts

1. Alfred Nobel
   - ❏ a. invented dynamite.
   - ❏ b. did important work in mathematics.
   - ❏ c. won the first Nobel Prize.

2. Alfred Nobel's will specified that
   - ❏ a. there be a prize for the study of plant life.
   - ❏ b. prizewinners had to live in Europe.
   - ❏ c. there be five prizes.

3. The Bank of Sweden added a prize in
   - ❏ a. economics.
   - ❏ b. history.
   - ❏ c. mathematics.

4. Today, a Nobel Prize in one category can be awarded to
   - ❏ a. only one person.
   - ❏ b. no more than three people.
   - ❏ c. any number of people.

5. People who have won two Nobel Prizes include
   - ❏ a. Albert Einstein and Linus Pauling.
   - ❏ b. Albert Einstein and Marie Curie.
   - ❏ c. Linus Pauling and Marie Curie.

Understanding Ideas

6. One can infer that one of Alfred Nobel's goals was to
   - ❏ a. help create weapons to help countries conquer other countries.
   - ❏ b. make the world a better place.
   - ❏ c. give all of his money to scientists.

7. A Nobel Prize winner is least likely to be
   - ❏ a. a writer.
   - ❏ b. a doctor.
   - ❏ c. an actor.

8. One can assume that a person who has won a Nobel Prize
   - ❏ a. is a scientist.
   - ❏ b. is creative and curious.
   - ❏ c. has made a great discovery.

9. One can infer that the most common reason Nobel Prizes have not been awarded in some years is that
   - ❏ a. the judges decided that no important work had been done in a particular category.
   - ❏ b. no one was nominated for an award.
   - ❏ c. there was not enough money to give to a winner.

10. One can assume from reading the article that Alfred Nobel most likely thought that
    - ❏ a. literature was more important than medicine.
    - ❏ b. the most important discoveries were in physics.
    - ❏ c. there were many ways in which a person could help humanity.

Doctors Without Borders

In 1999 the Nobel Peace Prize was awarded to a French organization called Doctors Without Borders. The judges who awarded the prize commended the group for "its pioneering work in providing medical care and humanitarian aid to victims of disasters on several continents."

Doctors Without Borders was founded in 1971. A group of doctors had become frustrated with the difficulties of trying to provide medical care in countries experiencing wars, epidemics, or natural disasters. These doctors often had trouble with government regulations and international laws that restricted their activities. They decided that they would make the welfare of victims their top priority, even if it meant ignoring regulations.

In its more than 30 years of existence, Doctors Without Borders has helped people in many parts of the world. Currently the group provides assistance in more than 80 countries. More than 2,500 people volunteer to work for the organization, and these people hire local people to help them in the regions where they work. Members of the group do not hesitate to speak out when they feel that their patients are being treated unfairly. They wish to make the world aware of the causes of suffering so that these causes can be eliminated. The group strives to avoid discrimination of any kind and to remain independent of particular political or religious beliefs.

1. Recognizing Words in Context

Find the word *commended* in the passage. One definition below is closest to the meaning of that word. One definition has the opposite or nearly opposite meaning. The remaining definition has a completely different meaning. Label the definitions C for *closest*, O for *opposite or nearly opposite*, and D for *different*.

_____ a. complimented

_____ b. criticized

_____ c. described

2. Distinguishing Fact from Opinion

Two of the statements below present *facts*, which can be proved correct. The other statement is an *opinion*, which expresses someone's thoughts or beliefs. Label the statements F for *fact* and O for *opinion*.

_____ a. Everyone should appreciate the work of Doctors Without Borders.

_____ b. Doctors Without Borders received the Nobel Peace Prize.

_____ c. Doctors Without Borders is based in France.

3. Keeping Events in Order

Label the statements below 1, 2, and 3 to show the order in which the events happened.

_____ a. Doctors Without Borders was founded.

_____ b. A group of doctors became frustrated with some government regulations.

_____ c. The size of the group's volunteer workforce grew to more than 2,500.

4. Making Correct Inferences

Two of the statements below are correct *inferences,* or reasonable guesses. They are based on information in the passage. The other statement is an incorrect, or faulty, inference. Label the statements C for *correct* inference and F for *faulty* inference.

_____ a. Doctors Without Border received more donations after winning the Nobel Peace Prize.

_____ b. Members of Doctors Without Borders sometimes say things that government leaders do not like.

_____ c. Doctors Without Borders makes large profits from its work.

5. Understanding Main Ideas

One of the statements below expresses the main idea of the passage. One statement is too general, or too broad. The other explains only part of the passage; it is too narrow. Label the statements M for *main idea,* B for *too broad,* and N for *too narrow.*

_____ a. Doctors Without Borders provides medical care for victims of wars and natural disasters.

_____ b. Doctors Without Borders avoids all types of discrimination.

_____ c. The Nobel Peace Prize is sometimes awarded to an organization.

Correct Answers, Part A _____

Correct Answers, Part B _____

Total Correct Answers _____

The human body is truly a wondrous machine. Inside it are billions of tiny units called cells, which perform the many actions needed to keep people alive. Day in and day out, the body is working. Even when a person is sleeping, the body still breathes and pumps blood to all of its parts. The way the body works is a mystery to most people, and scientists are only beginning to understand it.

The countless cells in the body are grouped into tissues. Each tissue has a purpose. For example, there are tissues that line the mouth, tissues that form muscles, and tissues that make up the heart. The heart is one example of a group of tissues called an organ.

An organ is simply a group of two or more kinds of tissue that has one main purpose. The heart's purpose is to pump blood throughout the body. All of the tissues in the heart work to pump blood. The heart is known as a vital organ because the body cannot survive without it. As the heart pumps, it moves blood rich in oxygen to all tissues. All other organs depend on the heart because they need oxygen to survive. They also depend, to different degrees, on other organs.

Organs that work together are called organ systems. One example of an organ system is the circulatory system. This system includes the heart, the blood, and the lungs. The lungs are involved in this system because they resupply the blood with oxygen while removing carbon dioxide. When the heart pumps blood into the lungs, the blood picks up oxygen and is then pumped to other tissues.

Another example of an organ system is the digestive system. This system changes the food that people eat into the energy that cells need to do their work. The system begins with two organs called the tongue and the esophagus. Food first enters the body through the mouth. After the food has been chewed, the tongue moves it into the esophagus. The esophagus is a long tube that pumps the food from the mouth to the stomach, another organ. Once in the stomach, food is stored until it is mixed with a digestive juice, which breaks it up into smaller pieces. The food then moves to the small intestine, where it is mixed with other juices. Any material that is not digested moves into the large intestine.

Reading Time _____

Recalling Facts

1. The body is made of billions of tiny units called
   - ❏ a. organs.
   - ❏ b. cells.
   - ❏ c. systems.

2. A group of cells that work together to serve a purpose is called a
   - ❏ a. tissue.
   - ❏ b. molecule.
   - ❏ c. bloodstream.

3. The digestive system is an example of
   - ❏ a. an organ.
   - ❏ b. an organ system.
   - ❏ c. a tissue.

4. A long tube that pumps food from the mouth to the stomach is called the
   - ❏ a. heart.
   - ❏ b. large intestine.
   - ❏ c. esophagus.

5. An organ consists of _____ or more types of tissues.
   - ❏ a. two
   - ❏ b. three
   - ❏ c. one

Understanding Ideas

6. People breathe and their hearts beat while they sleep, which means
   - ❏ a. most parts of the brain are wide awake at night.
   - ❏ b. some parts of the body are always working.
   - ❏ c. the blood contains more oxygen at night than it does during the day.

7. Which of the following statements is most likely true?
   - ❏ a. The tongue is the most important organ within the digestive system.
   - ❏ b. For an organ system to work properly, separate organs must do their jobs.
   - ❏ c. Scientists now know exactly how the human body works.

8. The article suggests that
   - ❏ a. every cell within the body depends on every other cell.
   - ❏ b. most people lack the digestive juices that break down food.
   - ❏ c. if one organ fails, other organs may not survive.

9. If a region of the body stopped receiving blood,
   - ❏ a. the tissues in the region would survive on stored oxygen for two or three weeks.
   - ❏ b. a heart attack would occur.
   - ❏ c. the cells, tissues, and organs within that region would die.

10. One can infer that a part of the body made up of one type of tissue
    - ❏ a. is an organ.
    - ❏ b. is not an organ.
    - ❏ c. has at least three kinds of cells.

The Importance of Water in the Body

Everyone knows that water is important to living creatures. In fact, without water, life on Earth would not exist. But why is water so important?

Water is vital to life because living creatures are made up mostly of water. The average human being is more than 60 percent water. This may seem surprising because people seem solid. But the inside of the human body is really quite fluid.

To visualize this, think about blood. There are about 4.7 liters (5 quarts) of blood in an adult body. Blood itself is very fluid. It is important for blood to be fluid because its task is to travel throughout the body, carrying oxygen and nutrients to the most distant regions. Without the liquid nature of blood, it would be impossible for the oxygen and nutrients to reach the entire body.

Water is such an important part of life that all living creatures must have it daily. The plants and animals that people rely on for food are made mainly of water. The chemical reactions that create nutrients for cells require water. Important bodily substances such as lymph, hormones, and urine are almost all water.

The world faces a serious water shortage. Some people have even fought wars over water. Better methods of conservation will be needed to prevent water shortages from becoming a worldwide crisis.

1. Recognizing Words in Context

Find the word *conservation* in the passage. One definition below is closest to the meaning of that word. One definition has the opposite or nearly opposite meaning. The remaining definition has a completely different meaning. Label the definitions C for *closest*, O for *opposite or nearly opposite,* and D for *different.*

_____ a. wasting

_____ b. saving

_____ c. sharing

2. Distinguishing Fact from Opinion

Two of the statements below present *facts,* which can be proved correct. The other statement is an *opinion,* which expresses someone's thoughts or beliefs. Label the statements F for *fact* and O for *opinion.*

_____ a. Life would not exist without water.

_____ b. The plants that people eat consist mainly of water.

_____ c. The blood with the most oxygen is the healthiest blood.

3. **Keeping Events in Order**

   Label the statements below 1, 2, and 3 to show the order in which the events happen.

   _____ a. Water enters the blood after it has been swallowed.

   _____ b. The blood carries water and nutrients to distant areas of the body.

   _____ c. A person drinks water.

4. **Making Correct Inferences**

   Two of the statements below are correct *inferences,* or reasonable guesses. They are based on information in the passage. The other statement is an incorrect, or faulty, inference. Label the statements C for *correct* inference and F for *faulty* inference.

   _____ a. All plants need water.

   _____ b. Bones do not contain water.

   _____ c. Food cannot be digested without water.

5. **Understanding Main Ideas**

   One of the statements below expresses the main idea of the passage. One statement is too general, or too broad. The other explains only part of the passage; it is too narrow. Label the statements M for *main idea,* B for *too broad,* and N for *too narrow.*

   _____ a. Water is essential to life.

   _____ b. The average person is more than 60 percent water.

   _____ c. Water is one of Earth's most important substances.

Correct Answers, Part A _____

Correct Answers, Part B _____

Total Correct Answers _____

Technology for People with Hearing or Visual Impairments

A person who has some hearing loss or who can't hear at all is said to have a hearing impairment. Modern technology can help people with hearing loss. Technology involves using science to make devices that do useful things.

Many people with some hearing loss wear hearing aids. A hearing aid is a small device that is powered by a battery. The hearing aid picks up sound waves and turns them into electrical signals. It sends the signals to speakers that turn them into sound loud enough for the person to hear. People with hearing impairments can communicate on the phone by using special keyboard devices that send and receive text messages over phone lines. When the phone rings, a light flashes.

Special alarms have been developed for people with hearing loss. A fire alarm makes a light flash when a person is awake and makes a pillow vibrate when the person is asleep. An alarm clock can have a flashing light or a loud buzzer, or it may cause the mattress to shake.

Thanks to technology, people with hearing loss can enjoy home entertainment. With closed captioning, they can watch TV or a movie. Captioning shows the actors' words in text on the screen.

Technology also can help people who are visually impaired. This means that the person has lost some sight or is blind. A screen reader lets a blind person use a computer. The screen reader reads the screen and speaks the words in a humanlike voice. Other programs magnify the print on the screen.

Braille is a means for enabling a person who is blind to read and write. Braille uses patterns of raised dots that can be read with the fingers. A Braillewriter is a machine that types in Braille. The user hits keys that make the dots on a special kind of paper. Talking note takers also use Braille. A student can take notes by typing on the device, which can read the notes aloud or print them in Braille.

A new technology for visually impaired people involves signs that talk. Small machines that send out signals are placed along streets or in buildings. A person uses a hand-held device to scan an area. For example, when pointed one way, the device might say "restroom." When pointed in another direction it might say "stairs." San Francisco is one of the cities that have these signs in place.

Reading Time _____

Recalling Facts

1. A hearing aid
   - ❏ a. changes sound waves into electrical signals.
   - ❏ b. gives a person perfect hearing.
   - ❏ c. is used only by older people.

2. A person with a hearing impairment can be warned about a fire by
   - ❏ a. the sound of fire engines.
   - ❏ b. the sound of a smoke detector.
   - ❏ c. a flashing light.

3. Braille
   - ❏ a. can magnify the words on a computer screen.
   - ❏ b. uses raised dots that can be read with the fingers.
   - ❏ c. is a kind of hearing aid.

4. Talking note takers
   - ❏ a. can read notes aloud or print them in Braille.
   - ❏ b. are used by the hearing impaired.
   - ❏ c. are used on telephones.

5. Signs that talk
   - ❏ a. are special fire alarms.
   - ❏ b. send out signals that are picked up by a hand-held device.
   - ❏ c. allow a person who is blind to use a computer.

Understanding Ideas

6. One can conclude from reading this article that
   - ❏ a. technology is much more helpful to people with hearing impairments than to people with visual impairments.
   - ❏ b. technology can help just a small percentage of people who have hearing loss.
   - ❏ c. there are many devices that make life easier for people with disabilities.

7. In the future, it is most likely that
   - ❏ a. all computers will print in Braille.
   - ❏ b. computers will have more features for people with disabilities.
   - ❏ c. guide dogs will no longer be needed.

8. A person who is deaf would benefit most from
   - ❏ a. a device that sends text messages over phone lines.
   - ❏ b. a hearing aid.
   - ❏ c. talking signs.

9. A person who is blind and wants to get around in a large city would be most helped by
   - ❏ a. talking signs.
   - ❏ b. a screen reader.
   - ❏ c. a hearing aid.

10. Of the following, the one that does not use technology is
    - ❏ a. a flashing fire alarm.
    - ❏ b. a talking watch.
    - ❏ c. sign language.

Learning Sign Language

Mr. Klein told the class that a new student, Inez, would be joining them soon. He said that Inez was deaf. She communicated by using sign language. Mr. Klein knew sign language, and he decided to teach his students so that they could also communicate with Inez.

First, they learned to sign the alphabet. Some letters were hard to remember. Other letters, such as *C*, were easier because the shape of the hand was similar to the shape of the letter. At first, some students' fingers moved awkwardly, but the students got better with practice.

The next thing they learned was fingerspelling. They signed one letter after another to spell a word. They started with two-letter words such as *at* and *on*. Then they spelled longer words.

Mr. Klein also taught the class how to sign numbers. To practice, they signed the answers to their math problems.

Finally, Mr. Klein showed that just one sign could be used for a whole word. To make the sign for the word *fine,* a person spreads out the fingers on one hand, touches the thumb to the chest, and moves the hand outward. Signing is not just done with the hands. Facial expressions are also important. The students learned to punctuate a question by raising their eyebrows.

When Inez first entered the classroom, she looked nervous. But the students signed, "Good morning, Inez." She gave the class a big smile and signed back, "What a wonderful welcome!"

1. **Recognizing Words in Context**

    Find the word *awkwardly* in the passage. One definition below is closest to the meaning of that word. One definition has the opposite or nearly opposite meaning. The remaining definition has a completely different meaning. Label the definitions C for *closest,* O for *opposite or nearly opposite,* and D for *different.*

    _____ a. in a careless way

    _____ b. in a clumsy way

    _____ c. in a skillful way

2. **Distinguishing Fact from Opinion**

    Two of the statements below present *facts,* which can be proved correct. The other statement is an *opinion,* which expresses someone's thoughts or beliefs. Label the statements F for *fact* and O for *opinion.*

    _____ a. It is difficult to learn sign language.

    _____ b. Mr. Klein knew sign language.

    _____ c. Fingerspelling is signing one letter after another to spell a word.

3. Keeping Events in Order

Label the statements below 1, 2, and 3 to show the order in which the events happened.

_____ a. Mr. Klein showed the class that just one sign can be used for a whole word.

_____ b. The class began learning to sign the alphabet.

_____ c. Mr. Klein told the class that a new student, Inez, would be joining them soon.

4. Making Correct Inferences

Two of the statements below are correct *inferences,* or reasonable guesses. They are based on information in the passage. The other statement is an incorrect, or faulty, inference. Label the statements C for *correct* inference and F for *faulty* inference.

_____ a. All signing is done using fingerspelling.

_____ b. Inez was pleased to find out that her classmates could communicate with her in sign language.

_____ c. Deaf people are not the only people who can learn sign language.

5. Understanding Main Ideas

One of the statements below expresses the main idea of the passage. One statement is too general, or too broad. The other explains only part of the passage; it is too narrow. Label the statements M for *main idea,* B for *too broad,* and N for *too narrow.*

_____ a. Mr. Klein taught his students to sign so that they could communicate with a new student.

_____ b. The students learned how to sign the alphabet.

_____ c. Deaf people can communicate in a number of ways.

Correct Answers, Part A _____

Correct Answers, Part B _____

Total Correct Answers _____

The Importance of Vitamins and Minerals

Vitamins and minerals are important parts of the human diet. The body needs these substances to grow and work properly. Vitamins help control the chemical reactions that create energy and living tissue. Minerals are needed for structures in the body to grow and work properly. They are also needed to create some important fluids, such as digestive juices. Many vitamins and minerals cannot be produced by the body. So humans must get them from the food they eat.

Some foods provide more vitamins and minerals than others do. Fruits and vegetables, for example, are full of vitamins. People who think they are not getting enough vitamins may take vitamins in the form of a pill. Taking vitamins in pill form is usually not harmful, but the best way to obtain vitamins is by eating a balanced diet.

Two of the best-known vitamins are vitamins C and E. These two vitamins are sometimes called antioxidants because they protect against tissue damage that can be caused by some oxygen compounds. Vitamin C also helps build strong bones and healthy blood vessels. Foods that are good sources of vitamin C include citrus fruits, strawberries, and tomatoes. Whole-grain foods are good sources of vitamin E and several B vitamins.

Another important vitamin is vitamin A. This vitamin keeps skin healthy, helps bones to grow, and works to fight infections. Eggs and milk contain vitamin A. Orange and dark green vegetables provide beta carotene, which the body can change into vitamin A. Vitamins A and E should not be consumed in extremely large amounts.

One of the most important minerals is calcium. Calcium is a mineral that people need for strong bones. If the body does not get enough calcium, it becomes vulnerable to a serious bone disease called osteoporosis. Milk and other dairy products are rich in calcium.

Other important minerals include magnesium, phosphorus, and potassium. Like calcium, magnesium and phosphorus are needed for strong bones. Whole-grain cereals are a good source of both. Potassium helps the body maintain proper fluid levels, and it helps muscles work properly. Bananas and oranges are good sources of potassium.

There are many other vitamins and minerals that are important for good health. Eating meals that consist of fresh foods rather than foods that come out of packages is the best way to get the vitamins and minerals a body needs. Eating poorly can cause serious health problems.

Reading Time _____

Recalling Facts

1. The best way to get enough vitamins and minerals is to
   - ❑ a. take multivitamin pills.
   - ❑ b. eat a balanced diet.
   - ❑ c. eat plenty of meat.

2. Among the most important vitamins are
   - ❑ a. A, C, and E.
   - ❑ b. C, K, and M.
   - ❑ c. A, E, and G.

3. One mineral that the body uses is
   - ❑ a. vitamin C.
   - ❑ b. potassium.
   - ❑ c. gold.

4. A good source of vitamin C is
   - ❑ a. chicken.
   - ❑ b. carrots.
   - ❑ c. strawberries.

5. A good source of calcium is
   - ❑ a. potatoes.
   - ❑ b. pork.
   - ❑ c. milk.

Understanding Ideas

6. From the information in the article, one can infer that vitamins and minerals are needed
   - ❑ a. mainly for strong bones.
   - ❑ b. for all parts of the body.
   - ❑ c. for skin and bones.

7. You can infer that _____ are among the most nutritious foods.
   - ❑ a. dark green vegetables
   - ❑ b. white breads and rolls
   - ❑ c. french fries and soft drinks

8. A person who does not like the sound of a dentist's drill should have lots of
   - ❑ a. milk.
   - ❑ b. meat.
   - ❑ c. potatoes.

9. According to the article, to build strong and healthy bones, people need
   - ❑ a. vitamins only.
   - ❑ b. minerals only.
   - ❑ c. both vitamins and minerals.

10. The article suggests that
    - ❑ a. only overweight people need to exercise.
    - ❑ b. one thing people can do to stay healthy is to eat lots of fruits and vegetables.
    - ❑ c. vitamins are more important than minerals are.

The Truth About Vitamin C

Vitamin C is vital for good health. Vitamin C promotes healthy teeth and gums, helps the body absorb iron, helps keep tissue healthy, and speeds the healing of wounds. It also helps the body fight off disease. The scientific name for vitamin C is ascorbic acid.

A person should eat foods that contain vitamin C every day, because the body is not able to store this vitamin. Many fruits and vegetables contain vitamin C.

A famous scientist named Linus Pauling claimed that large amounts of vitamin C could help prevent colds. He said that taking vitamin C every day had helped him avoid colds for many years. Scientific research has not shown any strong evidence to support Pauling's claim, although there is some evidence that vitamin C can ease the symptoms of a cold.

Research also shows that taking massive doses of vitamin C for long periods of time can be harmful. Some of the serious side effects are diarrhea and anemia, which is a shortage of red blood cells. But scientists emphasize that only very large amounts of vitamin C will cause problems. A person would have to take several vitamin C pills each day to reach this level.

People have also claimed that vitamin C can help prevent cancer. Research has not been able to support this claim. Nevertheless, vitamin C has many benefits, and eating foods that contain it promotes good health.

1. **Recognizing Words in Context**

   Find the word *promotes* in the passage. One definition below is closest to the meaning of that word. One definition has the opposite or nearly opposite meaning. The remaining definition has a completely different meaning. Label the definitions C for *closest,* O for *opposite or nearly opposite,* and D for *different.*

   _____ a. contributes to

   _____ b. prevents

   _____ c. affects

2. **Distinguishing Fact from Opinion**

   Two of the statements below present *facts,* which can be proved correct. The other statement is an *opinion,* which expresses someone's thoughts or beliefs. Label the statements F for *fact* and O for *opinion.*

   _____ a. Vitamin C is the most important vitamin.

   _____ b. Eating foods that are rich in vitamins is healthful.

   _____ c. There is no strong evidence that vitamin C prevents colds.

3. Keeping Events in Order

Label the statements below 1, 2, and 3 to show the order in which the events happened.

_____ a. A person eats foods rich in vitamin C.

_____ b. The symptoms of the cold are not severe.

_____ c. A person gets a cold.

4. Making Correct Inferences

Two of the statements below are correct *inferences,* or reasonable guesses. They are based on information in the passage. The other statement is an incorrect, or faulty, inference. Label the statements C for *correct* inference and F for *faulty* inference.

_____ a. Everyone who eats unhealthful food will get a cold at least once a year.

_____ b. Grapefruit is a good source of vitamin C.

_____ c. Some people who get enough vitamins will still get sick.

5. Understanding Main Ideas

One of the statements below expresses the main idea of the passage. One statement is too general, or too broad. The other explains only part of the passage; it is too narrow. Label the statements M for *main idea,* B for *too broad,* and N for *too narrow.*

_____ a. Massive doses of vitamin C taken for long periods of time can cause health problems.

_____ b. One type of vitamin is called vitamin C.

_____ c. Getting enough vitamin C keeps people healthy, but it does not prevent colds.

Correct Answers, Part A _____

Correct Answers, Part B _____

Total Correct Answers _____

Controlling body position is crucial to success in the sport of gymnastics. Gymnasts train a great deal to increase their strength and range of motion. The strength and flexibility allow them to hold poses and change positions on the floor as well as on apparatus that consists of such structures as bars, beams, and rings.

All the training in the world, however, would be useless to a gymnast without a sense of balance. It is a key to this sport. Balance is a natural process of the body that is controlled by the brain. The brain receives information from nerves throughout the body and uses it to direct movements that maintain balance. Joints, muscles, the skin, the eyes, and especially the inner ear also play a role in balance.

As a gymnast performs, the brain must tell the rest of the body in a split second what adjustments to make to maintain balance. It sends signals through the nerves to various muscles. The signals cause muscles to contract, or tighten. As a muscle contracts, it pulls on a bone and moves an arm or leg. The brain determines which bones move and how much they move.

Vaulting is one event in gymnastics that shows how nerves and the brain work together to control balance. When performing a vault, a gymnast first runs toward a springboard and jumps onto it. The springboard propels the gymnast toward a padded horizontal beam called a horse, which is about 1.2 meters (3 2/3 feet) high. As the gymnast comes off the board, the brain directs the arms and legs to the proper positions to maintain balance. Nerves along the joints and muscles send information to the brain about the body's position in the air. The brain then sends signals to make any necessary adjustments. The brain uses data from the eyes to control the precise placement of the hands on the horse. As the hands touch the horse, nerves in the skin give the brain more information about the body's placement, such as whether it is leaning to the left or the right. The brain instructs the hands to push off the horse and into the air, when the gymnast performs twists or other acrobatic movements. The gymnast must land standing up on a mat, which requires precise balance. The movement of liquid in the passageways of the inner ear creates nerve signals that help the brain rebalance the body.

Reading Time _____

Recalling Facts

1. Gymnasts train a great deal to increase their
   - ❑ a. height and muscle tone.
   - ❑ b. nerve sensitivity and brain chemistry.
   - ❑ c. strength and range of motion.

2. The part of the body that controls balance is
   - ❑ a. the spine.
   - ❑ b. the brain.
   - ❑ c. the eye.

3. Information about the body's placement is sent to the brain from
   - ❑ a. the ground.
   - ❑ b. nerves throughout the body.
   - ❑ c. heart muscles.

4. Equipment used in gymnastics includes
   - ❑ a. beams, bars, and rings.
   - ❑ b. ropes, hoops, and poles.
   - ❑ c. trapezes, tightropes, and nets.

5. The brain receives information from nerves in the inner ear on the basis of the position of
   - ❑ a. wax in the ear canal.
   - ❑ b. cells in the eardrum.
   - ❑ c. liquid in passageways.

Understanding Ideas

6. Gymnasts concentrate on developing muscles
   - ❑ a. in all parts of the body.
   - ❑ b. mainly in the legs.
   - ❑ c. mainly in the arms.

7. One can infer that as a gymnast trains over a long period of time, her or his sense of balance
   - ❑ a. stays about the same.
   - ❑ b. gets a little bit worse.
   - ❑ c. improves.

8. It is likely that the most dangerous part of a vault is when the gymnast
   - ❑ a. is running up to the springboard.
   - ❑ b. is touching the horse.
   - ❑ c. is landing on the mat.

9. One can infer that the entire process of performing one vault takes
   - ❑ a. one second.
   - ❑ b. several seconds.
   - ❑ c. close to a minute.

10. To maintain balance during vaulting, the brain relies on information from
    - ❑ a. only the inner ear.
    - ❑ b. only the arms and legs.
    - ❑ c. several parts of the body.

Training to Be a Gymnast

Gymnastics is a sport that requires a wide range of motion and a great deal of strength. A gymnast needs to be strong and flexible to create and hold the body shapes the sport is known for. Young gymnasts train to improve strength and range of motion while they learn basic body shapes.

During training, gymnasts spend a great deal of time stretching. Stretches are designed to help gymnasts hold body shapes with ease. Gymnasts do body tension drills too. For these drills, a gymnast holds a still pose while contracting a group of muscles. The gymnast tightens the muscles and then relaxes them, again and again.

Before gymnasts train on equipment, they learn the basic body shapes and movements while training on the floor. Two important shapes are the split and the bridge. In a split, the gymnast sits on the floor with the legs pointed in opposite directions. In a bridge, the gymnast lies on her or his back and pushes up with the hands so that the back is bent in an arc. Gymnasts also practice rolls, headstands, handstands, cartwheels, and still poses called balances. In each, gymnasts strive for precise form. Once the gymnasts have mastered these positions on the floor, they begin to use them off the ground on beams, horses, and other gymnastics apparatus.

1. **Recognizing Words in Context**

   Find the word *arc* in the passage. One definition below is closest to the meaning of that word. One definition has the opposite or nearly opposite meaning. The remaining definition has a completely different meaning. Label the definitions C for *closest,* O for *opposite or nearly opposite,* and D for *different.*

   _____ a. a curved line

   _____ b. a long line

   _____ c. a straight line

2. **Distinguishing Fact from Opinion**

   Two of the statements below present *facts,* which can be proved correct. The other statement is an *opinion,* which expresses someone's thoughts or beliefs. Label the statements F for *fact* and O for *opinion.*

   _____ a. Gymnasts spend time stretching.

   _____ b. Gymnasts learn basic body shapes.

   _____ c. Training to be a gymnast is hard work.

3. Keeping Events in Order

Label the statements below 1, 2, and 3 to show the order in which the events happen.

_____ a. A gymnast does a split on a balance beam.

_____ b. A gymnast gets on a balance beam for the first time.

_____ c. A gymnast trains on the floor to learn precise body shapes and movements.

4. Making Correct Inferences

Two of the statements below are correct *inferences, or* reasonable guesses. They are based on information in the passage. The other statement is an incorrect, or faulty, inference. Label the statements C for *correct* inference and F for *faulty* inference.

_____ a. Gymnasts sometimes get injured while training on gymnastics apparatus.

_____ b. The split and the bridge are the most common positions in gymnastics.

_____ c. Form is an important part of gymnastics.

5. Understanding Main Ideas

One of the statements below expresses the main idea of the passage. One statement is too general, or too broad. The other explains only part of the passage; it is too narrow. Label the statements M for *main idea*, B for *too broad,* and N for *too narrow.*

_____ a. Stretching improves strength and range of motion.

_____ b. Gymnasts train for their sport by developing strength and range of motion.

_____ c. Gymnastics requires a strong, flexible body.

Correct Answers, Part A _____

Correct Answers, Part B _____

Total Correct Answers _____

Gardening can be an interesting and enjoyable activity. Some helpful steps can make it easier to grow seeds in a garden.

Step One: Find out which plants will grow best in your area. For example, some plants that thrive in California don't survive in Michigan. Ask some successful gardeners in the neighborhood which plants grow well for them. Look in gardening books for suggestions. Make a list of interesting plants that are well suited to your area. Next to each plant, write the growing conditions it requires.

Step Two: Examine the growing conditions of your garden. Is the soil light and sandy or heavy with lots of clay? How much sunshine does the garden get? Choose the plants from the list that need the kind of soil and the amount of sunshine the garden provides. For example, impatiens are flowers that grow best in shade. Geraniums grow best in full sun.

Step Three: Buy seeds that were packaged for this year's planting.

Step Four: Determine the best time of the year to plant. In some southern states, it is possible to plant at various times of the year. In northern states, plant in the spring as soon as it is warm enough and there is little danger of frost. In places where the growing season is short, plant the seeds indoors in cups of soil and place the cups on a windowsill that receives sunlight. Tomatoes, peppers, zinnias, and marigolds can be grown for a few weeks indoors and then transplanted outdoors when the weather gets warmer.

Step Five: Prepare the garden by breaking up any clumps of dirt that are in the soil. Add rich compost or fertilizer and work it into the soil. Then rake the soil smooth.

Step Six: Plant the seeds in rows. Read the directions on the seed packages to find out how deep and far apart the seeds should be.

Step Seven: Keep the soil moist until the seeds sprout. Then water the plants as often and as much as needed. For example, zinnias do not need to be watered often. However, they need to be watered deeply, so that the water can seep down to the deepest roots. Other plants, like begonias, need to be watered lightly every other day. As the plants grow, remove any weeds that appear nearby.

Step Eight: To encourage new flowers to grow, pinch off the old ones when they are done blooming.

Reading Time _____

Recalling Facts

1. A good way to find out which plants will grow best in a garden is to
   - ❏ a. plant many kinds of seeds and see what happens.
   - ❏ b. ask successful gardeners in the neighborhood.
   - ❏ c. make a list of the plants you like.

2. Important conditions in a garden include all of the following except
   - ❏ a. the type of soil.
   - ❏ b. the age of garden tools.
   - ❏ c. the amount of sunshine.

3. In the northern states, seeds should be planted
   - ❏ a. in dry soil.
   - ❏ b. at different times of the year.
   - ❏ c. in the spring as soon as it is warm enough.

4. Before seeds have sprouted, gardeners should
   - ❏ a. keep the soil moist at all times.
   - ❏ b. water the soil every other day.
   - ❏ c. water the soil deeply once a week.

5. When seeds are planted indoors in cups of soil, the cups should be put
   - ❏ a. on a table in the middle of a room.
   - ❏ b. in a warm, dark basement.
   - ❏ c. on a windowsill.

Understanding Ideas

6. To grow plants from seeds, it is most important for a gardener to
   - ❏ a. plant them in rows.
   - ❏ b. start growing them in cups.
   - ❏ c. choose plants that grow well in his or her part of the country.

7. In a place that is warm year-round, gardeners
   - ❏ a. can plant seeds outside anytime that conditions are good.
   - ❏ b. should plant seeds only in the spring.
   - ❏ c. must plant seeds inside first and then later move the plants outside.

8. From reading this article, one can conclude that for seeds to sprout, they must have
   - ❏ a. expensive chemical fertilizers.
   - ❏ b. shelter from the wind.
   - ❏ c. moisture and warmth.

9. From the context of the article, one can infer that the word *transplanted* means
   - ❏ a. put a plant in different soil.
   - ❏ b. added pollen to a plant.
   - ❏ c. put seeds in a garden.

10. A gardener who plants seeds outdoors in October most likely lives in
    - ❏ a. Michigan.
    - ❏ b. California.
    - ❏ c. Alaska.

Wind, water, and animals carry seeds. Some seeds are light enough to float through the air. Dandelion, cottonwood, and milkweed seeds are attached to clusters of silky fibers that can travel for several kilometers on a windy day. The seeds of some maple trees are shaped like little wings. They whirl through the air and land a short distance from the tree.

Some trees, such as the coconut palm, rely on water to disperse their seeds. In many places, coconut trees grow near the ocean. During a storm, the tree bends in the wind. The coconuts may blow off and land in the ocean. The coconuts are carried by the waves, and some wash up on beaches and start new trees.

Sometimes animals transport seeds. A squirrel may pick up a nut and bury it someplace else. If the squirrel never digs the nut up, the nut may grow into a tree. Birds eat berries that have tiny seeds. The seeds pass through the birds' stomachs and land in other places in droppings. Raccoons and other animals eat fruit, such as apples. The animal may carry the fruit away to a different location, eat it, and leave some of the seeds. Some plants grow seeds inside burrs that stick to the fur of passing animals. The animals carry the seeds away, and the seeds fall off somewhere else.

1. Recognizing Words in Context

Find the word *disperse* in the passage. One definition below is closest to the meaning of that word. One definition has the opposite or nearly opposite meaning. The remaining definition has a completely different meaning. Label the definitions C for *closest*, O for *opposite or nearly opposite*, and D for *different*.

_____ a. gather together

_____ b. spread around

_____ c. plant again

2. Distinguishing Fact from Opinion

Two of the statements below present *facts*, which can be proved correct. The other statement is an *opinion*, which expresses someone's thoughts or beliefs. Label the statements F for *fact* and O for *opinion*.

_____ a. Some maple seeds are shaped like little wings.

_____ b. Cottonwood fibers can made a yard ugly.

_____ c. Animals transport some kinds of seeds.

3. **Keeping Events in Order**

   Label the statements below 1, 2, and 3 to show the order in which the events happen.

   _____ a. An ocean current carries along the coconut for several days.

   _____ b. A coconut sprouts on a different island.

   _____ c. A coconut falls off a tree and rolls down a beach and into the ocean.

4. **Making Correct Inferences**

   Two of the statements below are correct *inferences*, or reasonable guesses. They are based on information in the passage. The other statement is an incorrect, or faulty, inference. Label the statements C for *correct* inference and F for *faulty* inference.

   _____ a. Plants are less likely to become extinct if their seeds grow in many places.

   _____ b. The winglike shape of maple seeds causes them to be spread out over a larger area.

   _____ c. All coconuts are transported by the ocean.

5. **Understanding Main Ideas**

   One of the statements below expresses the main idea of the passage. One statement is too general, or too broad. The other explains only part of the passage; it is too narrow. Label the statements M for *main idea*, B for *too broad*, and N for *too narrow*.

   _____ a. Seeds come in different shapes and sizes.

   _____ b. Seeds are transported by wind, water, and animals.

   _____ c. Dandelion seeds can float through the air.

Correct Answers, Part A _____

Correct Answers, Part B _____

Total Correct Answers _____

Precipitation is defined as any water that falls from the atmosphere. This water can take different forms, including rain, snow, hail, and sleet.

Rain consists of drops of water that fall from clouds. Warm air picks up tiny drops of moisture from Earth's oceans, lakes, rivers, and streams. This moisture is called water vapor. Warm air tends to rise; and as it rises, it cools. Since cool air cannot hold as much moisture as warm air, the water vapor attaches to bits of dust or pollen and forms droplets. These droplets form clouds. As more and more water vapor attaches to the droplets, they become too heavy to float in the air, and they fall as rain.

If the temperature is very cold, the water vapor freezes around the bits of dust or pollen and forms crystals. As more and more water vapor freezes onto the crystals, they grow into snowflakes. When the snowflakes get heavy enough, they fall to the ground.

A single snowflake can contain up to 200 crystals. There are four basic shapes of snow crystals. One looks like a long needle. This type of crystal forms only high in the atmosphere where the air is coldest. The other three shapes each have six sides. One looks like a hollow column, another looks like a flat hexagon, and the third looks like a star. The shape of a crystal depends on the temperature and humidity at which the crystal forms. All snow crystals are symmetrical; that is, if you cut the crystal in half, each half will be a mirror image of the other.

Hail consists of balls of ice that form in layers. Within storm clouds are wind currents that flow upward. These winds carry water droplets up to colder air, where they freeze into ice particles. As the ice particles begin to fall, the wind currents may push them back up again. Layers of ice continue to form on the ice particles until balls of ice form. Eventually these balls become too heavy for the upward winds to lift them. They become hailstones and fall to the ground. Most hailstones are smaller than a dime, but sometimes they can be much larger.

Sleet forms when rain travels through very cold air near the ground and becomes partly frozen. Sleet can form a dangerous coating of ice on roads, windshields, and telephone wires.

Reading Time _____

Recalling Facts

1. Precipitation is
   - ❑ a. wind that carries water vapor.
   - ❑ b. any group of clouds very high in the atmosphere.
   - ❑ c. any form of water that falls from the atmosphere.

2. Rain consists of
   - ❑ a. drops of water that fall from clouds.
   - ❑ b. water vapor.
   - ❑ c. droplets that form a cloud.

3. Three of the four types of ice crystals
   - ❑ a. are shaped like needles.
   - ❑ b. are six-sided and symmetrical.
   - ❑ c. have liquid water trapped inside.

4. Hail consists of
   - ❑ a. clumps of snowflakes.
   - ❑ b. balls of ice that are formed in layers.
   - ❑ c. fog that freezes.

5. Sleet forms when
   - ❑ a. rain hits very cold air near the ground and becomes partly frozen.
   - ❑ b. air near the ground can hold no more water vapor.
   - ❑ c. snow melts in a cloud.

Understanding Ideas

6. One can conclude from reading this article that
   - ❑ a. water moves from Earth into the atmosphere and back to Earth, over and over.
   - ❑ b. the ocean is losing too much water into the air and is gradually drying up.
   - ❑ c. lakes are made of water vapor.

7. One can assume from reading this article that all forms of precipitation
   - ❑ a. fall from clouds.
   - ❑ b. have the same or nearly the same temperature.
   - ❑ c. contain bits of dust and pollen.

8. Very high clouds are more likely to be made of
   - ❑ a. water droplets.
   - ❑ b. ice crystals.
   - ❑ c. sleet.

9. If hail the size of golf balls began to fall, one could infer that
   - ❑ a. the hail formed in clouds with very strong upward wind currents.
   - ❑ b. wind pushed hailstones together as they fell from the sky.
   - ❑ c. huge hailstones exploded high in the atmosphere.

10. Tree branches are most likely to break when they are covered with large amounts of
    - ❑ a. snow.
    - ❑ b. rain.
    - ❑ c. sleet.

When air contains more water vapor than it can hold, water droplets form on cool objects that the air touches. These droplets are called condensation. The temperature at which condensation begins to form is called the dew point.

The following experiment shows how the dew point is measured. The materials needed are a metal can, water that is at room temperature, a thermometer, and ice cubes.

Step One: Place the can on a table in the middle of a room. Fill the can about two-thirds full of water.

Step Two: Place the thermometer in the water. Read the temperature.

Step Three: Add two or three ice cubes to the water. Watch the thermometer. Slowly add more ice until condensation begins to form on the outside of the can. Read the temperature. This is the dew point.

At the start of the experiment, the water was the same temperature as the air in the room. Then the ice made the water, and also the can, colder. The can cooled the adjacent air. As air gets cooler it cannot hold as much water vapor. When the air cooled to the point where it could no longer hold all of its water vapor, condensation formed.

Step Four: Repeat the experiment on a warm, sunny windowsill. The dew point will be different. This is because the air on the windowsill is warmer than the air in the middle of the room.

1. **Recognizing Words in Context**

Find the word *adjacent* in the passage. One definition below is closest to the meaning of that word. One definition has the opposite or nearly opposite meaning. The remaining definition has a completely different meaning. Label the definitions C for *closest*, O for *opposite or nearly opposite*, and D for *different*.

_____ a. distant

_____ b. nearby

_____ c. dry

2. **Distinguishing Fact from Opinion**

Two of the statements below present *facts*, which can be proved correct. The other statement is an *opinion*, which expresses someone's thoughts or beliefs. Label the statements F for *fact* and O for *opinion*.

_____ a. The middle of a room is the best place to measure dew point.

_____ b. When the air has more water than it can hold, condensation forms.

_____ c. As air cools, it cannot hold as much water.

3. **Keeping Events in Order**

   Label the statements below 1, 2, and 3 to show the order in which the steps should be performed.

   _____ a. Add ice cubes to the water.

   _____ b. Place the thermometer in the room-temperature water.

   _____ c. Fill the can about two-thirds full of water.

4. **Making Correct Inferences**

   Two of the statements below are correct *inferences,* or reasonable guesses. They are based on information in the passage. The other statement is an incorrect, or faulty, inference. Label the statements C for *correct* inference and F for *faulty* inference.

   _____ a. Warm air can hold more water than cold air can.

   _____ b. The dew point changes as certain conditions change.

   _____ c. The dew point is the same as the air temperature in a room.

5. **Understanding Main Ideas**

   One of the statements below expresses the main idea of the passage. One statement is too general, or too broad. The other explains only part of the passage; it is too narrow. Label the statements M for *main idea,* B for *too broad,* and N for *too narrow.*

   _____ a. Air that is very cold cannot hold much water.

   _____ b. Condensation is an important topic in the science of weather.

   _____ c. A classroom experiment can be used to find the dew point.

Correct Answers, Part A _____

Correct Answers, Part B _____

Total Correct Answers _____

When we say that an apple is red or a leaf is green, we mean that each appears to be these colors when seen in ordinary light. The way an object reflects and absorbs light determines its color.

The concept of light has proved to be very challenging for scientists. Light is energy that sometimes behaves likes waves and sometimes behaves like particles. When people use the word *light,* they are usually referring to electromagnetic energy that can be seen by the human eye.

Light behaves like waves when it produces colors. White light—such as sunlight—contains a mixture of colors. Each color of light has a different wavelength, or distance between waves. When a person shines a beam of white light through a piece of glass called a prism, the glass bends the waves at different angles. The result is a rainbow of colors—red, orange, yellow, green, blue, indigo, and violet. This range of colors is known as the spectrum. Red is the color of the spectrum with the longest wavelength, and violet is the color with the shortest.

When light strikes an object, some wavelengths of light are absorbed. Others are reflected. An object appears a certain color because of the color of light it reflects. A leaf looks green because it reflects the green light. An apple looks red because it reflects the red light. Some objects absorb all colors of light, and some absorb none. An object that appears black absorbs all colors of light. None are reflected. On the other hand, an object that appears white reflects all colors of light. None are absorbed.

The relationship between light and color can be seen by viewing a red apple in blue light. In this light, the apple does not look red because there is no red light for the apple to reflect. Because the apple's skin absorbs all other colors of light, the apple looks black.

A few substances, such as glass and water, do not reflect much light. Some wavelengths of light travel through these materials, and other wavelengths are absorbed. Red stained glass, for example, allows red light to pass through it and absorbs all other colors. When sunlight shines on ocean water, a different process takes place. The light strikes tiny particles in the water and is scattered, or reflected in many directions. Blue light scatters more intensely than other colors, so the water usually appears blue.

Reading Time _____

Recalling Facts

1. When a beam of white light passes through a prism, the light is bent to reveal
   - ❑ a. its speed.
   - ❑ b. its brightness.
   - ❑ c. the spectrum.

2. An object appears a certain color because of the color of light it
   - ❑ a. absorbs.
   - ❑ b. reflects.
   - ❑ c. produces.

3. An object that absorbs all colors of light appears
   - ❑ a. black.
   - ❑ b. white.
   - ❑ c. blue.

4. The ocean appears blue because
   - ❑ a. water is always blue.
   - ❑ b. sunlight is yellow.
   - ❑ c. water scatters blue light most intensely.

5. The color of light is determined by its
   - ❑ a. wavelength.
   - ❑ b. brightness.
   - ❑ c. number of watts.

Understanding Ideas

6. You can infer from the information in the article that a banana appears yellow because it
   - ❑ a. absorbs yellow light.
   - ❑ b. absorbs all light.
   - ❑ c. reflects yellow light.

7. You can infer that fruit punch appears red because
   - ❑ a. the punch reflects all other colors.
   - ❑ b. the punch scatters red light most intensely.
   - ❑ c. the punch does not absorb any light.

8. It is likely that a black object placed in sunlight will become hotter than a white object because
   - ❑ a. the wavelength of black light is longest.
   - ❑ b. black absorbs white light, whereas white reflects it.
   - ❑ c. light passes through the black object.

9. You can infer that the deepest parts of the ocean are dark because as light passes through hundreds of meters of water
   - ❑ a. only black light is not absorbed.
   - ❑ b. none of the light is absorbed.
   - ❑ c. all colors of light are eventually absorbed.

10. The article suggests that all color in the world is the result of
    - ❑ a. light.
    - ❑ b. paints.
    - ❑ c. dyes.

Primary Colors of Paint and Light

The science of mixing colors is integral to the visual arts. Painters can create any color by mixing just three colors of paint. Every image on a television or computer screen is made up of only three colors of light.

The three colors that make up all other colors are called primary colors. You may have been taught in art class that the primary colors are blue, red, and yellow. Actually, scientists refer to the primary color of blue as cyan, and they refer to the primary color of red as magenta, so the primary colors of paint are cyan, magenta, and yellow. When equal amounts of any two primary colors are mixed, a secondary color is created. For paint, the secondary colors are orange, green, and purple.

For light, the three primary colors are different. They are red, green, and blue. When two primary colors of light are mixed, a secondary color is created, just as with paint. But for light the secondary colors are cyan, magenta, and yellow. A combination of blue and red light produces magenta light. A combination of blue and green light produces cyan light. A combination of red and green light produces yellow light.

The reason that the primary colors are different for paint and light is that paint contains pigments. Pigments absorb light, so a person sees only the wavelengths of light that are not absorbed.

1. **Recognizing Words in Context**

   Find the word *integral* in the passage. One definition below is closest to the meaning of that word. One definition has the opposite or nearly opposite meaning. The remaining definition has a completely different meaning. Label the definitions C for *closest*, O for *opposite or nearly opposite*, and D for *different*.

   _____ a. essential

   _____ b. unnecessary

   _____ c. larger

2. **Distinguishing Fact from Opinion**

   Two of the statements below present *facts*, which can be proved correct. The other statement is an *opinion*, which expresses someone's thoughts or beliefs. Label the statements F for *fact* and O for *opinion*.

   _____ a. Primary colors make up all other colors.

   _____ b. Artists are the best judges of how to use colors.

   _____ c. Small dots of light form television images.

3. Keeping Events in Order

Label the statements below 1, 2, and 3 to show the order in which the events happen.

_____ a. A painter paints the first wildflower.

_____ b. A painter mixes yellow and magenta paint to create orange.

_____ c. A painter decides to paint a meadow covered with orange wildflowers.

4. Making Correct Inferences

Two of the statements below are correct *inferences,* or reasonable guesses. They are based on information in the passage. The other statement is an incorrect, or faulty, inference. Label the statements C for *correct* inference and F for *faulty* inference.

_____ a. Mixing cyan and magenta paint produces a different color from that produced by mixing cyan and magenta light.

_____ b. The primary colors of paint and the secondary colors of light are the same three colors.

_____ c. Mixing the three primary colors of paint produces a very light color.

5. Understanding Main Ideas

One of the statements below expresses the main idea of the passage. One statement is too general, or too broad. The other explains only part of the passage; it is too narrow. Label the statements M for *main idea,* B for *too broad,* and N for *too narrow.*

_____ a. The primary colors of paint are different from the primary colors of light.

_____ b. All colors are the result of light.

_____ c. Cyan, magenta, and yellow are the primary colors of paint.

Correct Answers, Part A _____

Correct Answers, Part B _____

Total Correct Answers _____

How Humans Hear

Everything that humans hear is in the form of waves. Just as the eye sees light waves in the form of colors, the ear hears sound waves in the form of noises. The ear and the eye translate these different waves into nerve signals that the brain can make sense of. The hearing process consists of several steps.

Sound waves are created when something vibrates in the air. For example, if you drop a fork on a table, the fork vibrates and creates sound waves. Sound waves are absorbed by a part of the ear called the eardrum. As the sound hits the eardrum, it sets off a chain reaction. The eardrum vibrates, creating movements in a group of small bones. The bones are attached to the cochlea, a structure that is shaped like a snail's shell. The movements of the small bones create motion in a liquid within the cochlea. The liquid covers small hairs called cilia, which move whenever the liquid moves. The cilia are attached to nerve cells that send signals to the brain. The brain analyzes these signals and identifies the sound that created them.

The ears and brain have a remarkable ability to recognize particular sounds. For example, a mother often can tell when her baby is crying even if there are other crying babies in the same room. This is because the sound of her baby's cry has special meaning to her and the brain has recorded its importance.

The ability to recognize sounds improves with experience. As the brain receives information about sounds from day to day, it stores the information in its memory. When the brain hears new sounds, it assigns meaning to them based on the information already in the memory. This is why certain words or songs can make a person happy. Often it is not the words or songs themselves that cause this feeling. The sounds are linked to happy memories for that person.

Another hearing process controlled by the brain involves determining where a sound is coming from. One ear is usually closer to the source of a sound than the other ear is. Sound waves are stronger when they reach the ear that is closer. They also reach the closer ear first. A part of the brain called the sensory cortex recognizes these differences and uses them to determine the location of the source of the sound.

Reading Time _____

Recalling Facts

1. Both sound and light
   - ❑ a. are carried in electrical currents.
   - ❑ b. have wavelike forms.
   - ❑ c. create nerve signals in the cochlea.

2. The cochlea contains
   - ❑ a. mostly blood.
   - ❑ b. only air.
   - ❑ c. liquid.

3. _____ lies between the eardrum and the cochlea.
   - ❑ a. A group of small bones
   - ❑ b. A line of cilia
   - ❑ c. Empty space

4. The location of the source of a sound is determined by a section of the brain called the
   - ❑ a. brain stem.
   - ❑ b. sensory cortex.
   - ❑ c. spinal cord.

5. Sounds waves are created by
   - ❑ a. nerve signals.
   - ❑ b. vibrations in the air.
   - ❑ c. movements of the eardrum.

Understanding Ideas

6. One can conclude from the article that sounds that make a person happy or sad often do so because of the person's
   - ❑ a. experiences.
   - ❑ b. taste in music.
   - ❑ c. intelligence.

7. The article suggests that if a person's eardrums are badly damaged,
   - ❑ a. sound will simply bounce off it.
   - ❑ b. the brain will not be able to identify sounds.
   - ❑ c. the sensory cortex will stop working.

8. You can infer that the easiest sounds for a brain to recognize are those that
   - ❑ a. are loudest.
   - ❑ b. have been heard most often.
   - ❑ c. are the most pleasant.

9. A mother can probably recognize the sound of her baby's cry in a very loud room because
   - ❑ a. she knows that the cry means the baby is seriously ill.
   - ❑ b. the cry is much louder than all of the other sounds put together.
   - ❑ c. her brain has assigned great importance to that sound.

10. One can infer that if a person has lost the hearing in one ear, it will be most difficult for that person to identify
    - ❑ a. the loudness of a sound.
    - ❑ b. where a sound is coming from.
    - ❑ c. what is making a sound.

14 B — Sound-Wave Interference

Sound travels in waves through the air. In some ways, sound waves are similar to ocean waves. For instance, they change shape when they come into contact with other waves. When two sound waves meet, interference is the result.

Interference varies according to the type of sound waves. Interference can create new waves that are bigger or smaller than each of the original waves that combine. Each sound wave has a high and a low point. If the high points of two waves occur at the same time, bigger waves are created, and the sound is louder. This is called constructive interference. If the high point of one wave occurs at the same time as the low point of another wave, the sound is softer. This is called destructive interference.

If both waves are exactly the same size, and the top of one wave occurs at exactly the same time as the bottom of another wave, the sounds may completely cancel each other out and create silence. This rarely happens.

If the waves of one sound are longer than the waves of another sound, a different kind of interference may occur. Sometimes the tops of the two waves occur at the same time, and at other times the top of one wave occurs at the same time as the bottom of another wave. This can create an unpleasant sound, as when one musical instrument is out of tune with another.

1. **Recognizing Words in Context**

   Find the word *varies* in the passage. One definition below is closest to the meaning of that word. One definition has the opposite or nearly opposite meaning. The remaining definition has a completely different meaning. Label the definitions C for *closest,* O for *opposite or nearly opposite,* and D for *different.*

   _____ a. stays the same

   _____ b. vibrates quickly

   _____ c. changes

2. **Distinguishing Fact from Opinion**

   Two of the statements below present *facts,* which can be proved correct. The other statement is an *opinion,* which expresses someone's thoughts or beliefs. Label the statements F for *fact* and O for *opinion.*

   _____ a. It is amazing when two sound waves completely cancel each other out.

   _____ b. Some sound waves are longer than others are.

   _____ c. Destructive interference results in softer sounds.

3. Keeping Events in Order

Label the statements below 1, 2, and 3 to show the order in which the events happen.

_____ a. A trumpet begins to play.

_____ b. An unpleasant sound is created.

_____ c. Another trumpet begins to play, and it is out of tune.

4. Making Correct Inferences

Two of the statements below are correct *inferences,* or reasonable guesses. They are based on information in the passage. The other statement is an incorrect, or faulty, inference. Label the statements C for *correct* inference and F for *faulty* inference.

_____ a. Constructive interference almost never happens.

_____ b. Some car horns produce longer sound waves than other car horns do.

_____ c. Sound waves can have different heights.

5. Understanding Main Ideas

One of the statements below expresses the main idea of the passage. One statement is too general, or too broad. The other explains only part of the passage; it is too narrow. Label the statements M for *main idea,* B for *too broad,* and N for *too narrow.*

_____ a. Interference occurs when sound waves collide.

_____ b. Different sound waves produce different sounds.

_____ c. Destructive interference makes sounds softer.

Correct Answers, Part A _____

Correct Answers, Part B _____

Total Correct Answers _____

People have not always used numbers. It took thousands of years for people to invent number systems. In the earliest civilizations, peoples used tallies to keep track of how many of an item they had. Some people made marks on sticks and bones. Others made piles of beads or shells. Such methods worked well enough, because in ancient times people rarely dealt with large numbers of items.

Scholars believe that some ancient peoples counted by pointing to body parts. Different parts, such as fingers and elbows, stood for different numbers. Today, some peoples, such as the Paiela of Papua New Guinea, still count in this way. The largest number used by the Paiela is 28. They use this counting system while working in the fields or while trading goods.

When the first towns and villages began to appear, people needed more sophisticated ways to count. The farmers who lived in villages in one ancient Middle Eastern civilization used different sets of tokens to count different kinds of things. They used small disks to count sheep, but egg-shaped tokens were used to count jars of oil.

About 5,000 years ago, a new kind of number system appeared. The Sumerians, who lived in what is now Iraq, developed this system soon after they had developed one of the first systems of writing. In the Sumerian number system, the same set of marks was used to count every kind of thing. Other advanced ancient civilizations developed similar number systems. The Egyptians used a set of picture symbols in their system, and the Maya used a set of dots and dashes.

Number systems contributed to impressive accomplishments and a better way of life. The Egyptians used numbers in building and measuring the pyramids. They used numbers in trade, for farming, and to tell time too. Numbers helped the Maya to make one of the first accurate calendars.

The system of numbers used today in most parts of the world began in India in about the year A.D. 500. This system uses 10 numerals, from zero to nine. Their value depends on where they are placed in a number. Using place value has made it possible to do calculations with large numbers quickly. Scientific advances have created the need for very large and very small numbers. Recently, the name *googol* was created for a number that consists of one followed by one hundred zeros.

Reading Time _____

Recalling Facts

1. To tell how many of an item they had, people in the earliest civilizations used
   - ❏ a. clay tablets.
   - ❏ b. only the numbers 1–10.
   - ❏ c. tallies.

2. To count, farmers in some of the first villages used
   - ❏ a. different kinds of tokens.
   - ❏ b. marks on sticks.
   - ❏ c. computers.

3. About 5,000 years ago, the Sumerians invented a number system that used
   - ❏ a. body parts.
   - ❏ b. round disks.
   - ❏ c. one set of numbers to count all things.

4. A number system invented in India in about the year 500 is
   - ❏ a. no longer used.
   - ❏ b. used mainly in India.
   - ❏ c. used now in most of the world.

5. The need for large numbers is
   - ❏ a. decreasing.
   - ❏ b. increasing.
   - ❏ c. staying about the same.

Understanding Ideas

6. The article suggests that changes in counting methods have resulted from
   - ❏ a. changes in the way people live.
   - ❏ b. the increasing intelligence of human beings.
   - ❏ c. the creation of calculators and computers.

7. One disadvantage of using tokens to count sheep would be that
   - ❏ a. people might lose some of the tokens and become confused.
   - ❏ b. large herds of sheep would be difficult to count.
   - ❏ c. many sheep would run away.

8. Compared with the ancient use of numbers, the modern use of numbers has
   - ❏ a. led to a decline in trade.
   - ❏ b. made life more complex.
   - ❏ c. made it easier to perform calculations.

9. One can infer that the ancient Egyptians' number system helped them build the pyramids, because it
   - ❏ a. helped them to calculate the number of workers and amount of materials needed.
   - ❏ b. helped them to invent gasoline-powered equipment.
   - ❏ c. allowed them to use algebra to calculate area.

10. It would be difficult to count 100 items in a counting system based on the use of
    - ❏ a. body parts.
    - ❏ b. picture symbols.
    - ❏ c. the numerals zero to nine.

15 B   Using Geometry to Solve Everyday Problems

When the Wilsons decided to host a family reunion at a state park, Keisha and Brendan helped their parents prepare for it in an unusual way. Mrs. Wilson did not know how much liquid her new plastic container could hold. She wanted to measure its volume so that she would know how much lemonade to make. She asked the twins, who knew some geometry, to help. Geometry allows people to measure just about anything.

Using a ruler, the twins measured the container's base and then figured out its area. They multiplied that value by the height of the container to find the volume. They told their mother she could make up to 10 liters (11 quarts) of lemonade.

Next, the family filled a huge cooler with food for the reunion. The cooler was so ponderous that the parents and children had to drag the cooler along on the ground out to the truck. At the truck, a new problem arose. They were not able to lift the massive cooler onto the back of the pickup truck. Looking around, Mr. Wilson found some boards to use as a ramp. Using what they knew about angles, the twins chose a long board to make a ramp with a small angle. It was easy to push the cooler up the ramp. With the help of geometry, the family was ready for the big event.

1. **Recognizing Words in Context**

   Find the word *ponderous* in the passage. One definition below is closest to the meaning of that word. One definition has the opposite or nearly opposite meaning. The remaining definition has a completely different meaning. Label the definitions C for *closest*, O for *opposite or nearly opposite*, and D for *different*.

   _____ a. wide

   _____ b. light

   _____ c. heavy

2. **Distinguishing Fact from Opinion**

   Two of the statements below present *facts*, which can be proved correct. The other statement is an *opinion*, which expresses someone's thoughts or beliefs. Label the statements F for *fact* and O for *opinion*.

   _____ a. Geometry is the most useful type of math.

   _____ b. The volume of a cylinder can be found by multiplying its height by the area of its base.

   _____ c. The Wilsons use a ramp to get the cooler onto the truck.

3. **Keeping Events in Order**

   Label the statements below 1, 2, and 3 to show the order in which the events happen.

   _____ a. The area is multiplied by the container's height to find the volume.

   _____ b. Mrs. Wilson does not know the volume of her plastic container.

   _____ c. The twins find the area of the container's base.

4. **Making Correct Inferences**

   Two of the statements below are correct *inferences*, or reasonable guesses. They are based on information in the passage. The other statement is an incorrect, or faulty, inference. Label the statements C for *correct* inference and F for *faulty* inference.

   _____ a. Only a few people are expected to attend the family reunion.

   _____ b. Engineers use geometry when they design containers.

   _____ c. The twins have studied volume in geometry class.

5. **Understanding Main Ideas**

   One of the statements below expresses the main idea of the passage. One statement is too general, or too broad. The other explains only part of the passage; it is too narrow. Label the statements M for *main idea*, B for *too broad*, and N for *too narrow*.

   _____ a. Calculating the volume of a container involves calculating the area of its base.

   _____ b. Keisha and Brendan use geometry to help their parents prepare for a reunion.

   _____ c. Geometry can be used in many ways.

   Correct Answers, Part A _____

   Correct Answers, Part B _____

   Total Correct Answers _____

Venus: Earth's Sister Planet

For several reasons, Venus is often referred to as Earth's sister planet. Most of the time, Venus is the planet that is closest to Earth. Venus and Earth are about the same size. On both Earth and Venus, volcanic eruptions have produced rocky surfaces that are much younger than the planets themselves.

Thick clouds of carbon dioxide gas and sulfuric acid hide the surface of Venus. It is only in recent decades that scientists have been able to look underneath them. We now know that although Venus and Earth are alike in some ways, they are also very different. One major difference is that Earth has an atmosphere that supports life. On Venus, the temperature averages about 460 degrees Celsius (860 degrees Fahrenheit). This is even hotter than Mercury, which is the only planet that is closer to the Sun than Venus is. Venus is so hot because its dense, high-pressure atmosphere traps the Sun's heat. This is called a greenhouse effect. Scientists believe that Venus once had as much water as Earth. The water eventually boiled away due to Venus's intense heat.

Unlike Earth, Venus has no moon. Also, Venus rotates, or turns, east to west. Earth (and almost all the other planets) turn in the other direction. Venus rotates very slowly: it takes Venus 243 Earth days to make just one complete rotation. But it takes only 225 Earth days for Venus to make one trip around the Sun. This is because Venus is closer to the Sun than Earth is. The orbit of Venus is shaped almost exactly like a circle.

In 1962 *Mariner 2* became the first spacecraft to fly by Venus. This U.S. spacecraft was able to confirm the rotation rate of the planet. The Soviet Union landed several spacecraft on Venus during the 1970s and 1980s. They sent back photographs of the planet's surface. *Magellan,* another U.S. spacecraft, used radar to map most of the surface in 1989 and 1990. The photos and maps show that Venus is covered with rolling hills and broad plains.

Except for the Sun and the Moon, Venus is the brightest body that can be seen from Earth. At different times, it can be one of the first objects to appear in the night sky at twilight or one of the last to disappear at dawn. This is why it has been called both the morning star and the evening star.

Reading Time _____

Recalling Facts

1. Venus is
   - ❏ a. about the same size as Earth.
   - ❏ b. much larger than Earth.
   - ❏ c. much smaller than Earth.

2. Venus rotates
   - ❏ a. at the same speed as Earth.
   - ❏ b. much faster than Earth.
   - ❏ c. much more slowly than Earth.

3. Venus is extremely hot because
   - ❏ a. it is the closest planet to the Sun.
   - ❏ b. its dense atmosphere traps the Sun's heat.
   - ❏ c. it has no clouds to block the sun.

4. One of the main ingredients of Venus's atmosphere is
   - ❏ a. carbon dioxide gas.
   - ❏ b. oxygen gas.
   - ❏ c. water vapor.

5. Venus has
   - ❏ a. no moons.
   - ❏ b. one moon.
   - ❏ c. three moons.

Understanding Ideas

6. One can conclude that Venus and Earth are
   - ❏ a. more different than they are alike.
   - ❏ b. alike in almost every way.
   - ❏ c. not alike at all.

7. From the information in the article, one can infer that Venus is the
   - ❏ a. second closest planet to the Sun.
   - ❏ b. third closest planet to the Sun.
   - ❏ c. closest planet to the Sun.

8. The main reason that it would be difficult for astronauts to walk on Venus would be the
   - ❏ a. lack of oxygen in the atmosphere.
   - ❏ b. lack of water.
   - ❏ c. high temperature and high pressure.

9. One can infer that scientists did not have a good idea of what minerals are found on Venus's surface until
   - ❏ a. the invention of the telescope.
   - ❏ b. Soviet spacecraft landed on Venus.
   - ❏ c. the *Mariner 2* spacecraft flew by Venus.

10. It is likely that the material on the surface of Venus comes mainly from
    - ❏ a. meteorites.
    - ❏ b. lava.
    - ❏ c. sulfuric acid.

16   B   Galileo's Telescope

The Italian scientist Galileo Galilei made some of the most important discoveries in the history of astronomy. In 1609 Galileo heard about a new invention by a Dutch eyeglass maker. This invention, the telescope, consisted of two lenses in a tube. It made faraway objects appear larger. The first lens bent the light waves that entered the tube. This brought them to a point, forming an image. The second lens magnified the image. This first telescope could make an image seem three times larger. At once Galileo went to work to make a more powerful telescope. He needed stronger lenses, so he learned to make his own. He was able to produce powerful telescopes that could be used to view the night sky in greater detail.

Galileo's first important discovery in astronomy was that there were mountains on the Moon. People had previously believed that the Moon was a smooth sphere. Galileo's observations of the way that Venus appeared in the night sky caused a sensation. These observations helped prove that the Sun, and not Earth, was at the center of the solar system. Some people became very angry with Galileo for disagreeing with what had been accepted beliefs. Other important astronomical discoveries by Galileo included sunspots and the moons of Jupiter.

1. **Recognizing Words in Context**

   Find the word *sensation* in the passage. One definition below is closest to the meaning of that word. One definition has the opposite or nearly opposite meaning. The remaining definition has a completely different meaning. Label the definitions C for *closest*, O for *opposite or nearly opposite*, and D for *different*.

   _____ a. something that people find very interesting

   _____ b. something that people find very boring

   _____ c. something that people find very annoying

2. **Distinguishing Fact from Opinion**

   Two of the statements below present *facts*, which can be proved correct. The other statement is an *opinion*, which expresses someone's thoughts or beliefs. Label the statements F for *fact* and O for *opinion*.

   _____ a. Galileo learned to make his own telescope lenses.

   _____ b. Galileo saw mountains on the Moon.

   _____ c. Galileo was the greatest scientist of his time.

3. Keeping Events in Order

Label the statements below 1, 2, and 3 to show the order in which the events happened.

_____ a. In 1609 Galileo heard about a new invention.

_____ b. Galileo made his own telescope.

_____ c. Galileo studied the movement of Venus in the night sky.

4. Making Correct Inferences

Two of the statements below are correct *inferences,* or reasonable guesses. They are based on information in the passage. The other statement is an incorrect, or faulty, inference. Label the statements C for *correct* inference and F for *faulty* inference.

_____ a. Galileo made many important discoveries about astronomy.

_____ b. Galileo was the first to realize that Venus was a planet and not a star.

_____ c. Galileo did not believe everything that other scientists believed.

5. Understanding Main Ideas

One of the statements below expresses the main idea of the passage. One statement is too general, or too broad. The other explains only part of the passage; it is too narrow. Label the statements M for *main idea,* B for *too broad,* and N for *too narrow.*

_____ a. Galileo made important discoveries with his telescope.

_____ b. The invention of the telescope was one of the most important developments in the history of astronomy.

_____ c. Galileo discovered that Jupiter has moons.

Correct Answers, Part A _____

Correct Answers, Part B _____

Total Correct Answers _____

Reptiles are cold-blooded animals that have backbones. The term *cold-blooded* describes animals whose bodies stay the same temperature as their surroundings. Reptiles have lungs to breathe air, and their bodies are covered with tough scales or plates. Many are able to go without food for long periods of time. Most reptiles hatch from eggs. Some examples of reptiles are lizards, turtles, snakes, and crocodilians.

Lizards make up the largest group of reptiles. There are more than 3,000 kinds of lizards. Most lizards have four legs and a tail, but some have only tiny legs or no legs at all. These lizards look like snakes. Most lizards have claws, but the gecko has toes for climbing smooth surfaces with. Almost all lizards eat insects. A few eat other animals or plants.

A turtle is a toothless reptile with a hard shell that protects its body. When threatened, many turtles pull their heads and limbs into their shells. Most turtles live in marshes, swamps, and other bodies of fresh water. Others live in the ocean or on land. Turtles may eat plants, small animals, or both. Insects and worms are among the animals most often eaten by turtles. One small turtle, the box turtle, grows only to about 15 centimeters (6 inches) long. Leatherback sea turtles may grow up to 3.7 meters (12 feet) long. Some kinds of turtles live longer than any other animals, including humans.

Snakes have long, round bodies that are covered with scales. Having no legs, snakes move by wriggling along on the ground or stretching themselves between tree branches. Snakes have jaws with sharp teeth that may include poisonous fangs. Snakes swallow their prey whole and later spit out the undigested parts. One very large snake, the reticulated python, can eat animals that weigh as much as 70 kilograms (154 pounds).

The crocodilians are a group of reptiles that includes alligators and crocodiles. They are the largest reptiles and are closely related to birds. They also are considered to be the most direct descendants of dinosaurs. Crocodilians live in water and swim, using their long tails. They eat birds, fish, and other animals. They grab their prey in their strong jaws and crush it. Crocodilians can move on land by crawling or walking on their short legs. Crocodiles have narrower heads than alligators do. Crocodiles usually live in salt water, whereas alligators are most often found in fresh water.

Reading Time _____

Recalling Facts

1. The largest group of reptiles is made up of
   - ❑ a. crocodilians.
   - ❑ b. lizards.
   - ❑ c. snakes.

2. Crocodilians are closely related to
   - ❑ a. sharks.
   - ❑ b. worms.
   - ❑ c. birds.

3. Most reptiles
   - ❑ a. hatch from eggs.
   - ❑ b. are fed milk by their mothers when born.
   - ❑ c. ride on their mothers' backs when they are young.

4. The reptiles that live the longest are
   - ❑ a. turtles.
   - ❑ b. crocodiles.
   - ❑ c. lizards.

5. The largest reptiles are
   - ❑ a. pythons.
   - ❑ b. leatherneck turtles.
   - ❑ c. crocodilians.

Understanding Ideas

6. One can conclude from reading this article that
   - ❑ a. reptiles look very different but all have tails.
   - ❑ b. all reptiles look very similar and act in very similar ways.
   - ❑ c. reptiles can look different but share important characteristics.

7. One can infer that turtles
   - ❑ a. are cold-blooded.
   - ❑ b. can breathe while under water.
   - ❑ c. spend most of their time on land.

8. Fish lay eggs and have scales, but they are not like any reptiles because they
   - ❑ a. live only in the water.
   - ❑ b. have no legs.
   - ❑ c. do not have lungs with which to breathe air.

9. A lizard would be most likely to eat a
   - ❑ a. leaf.
   - ❑ b. mouse.
   - ❑ c. beetle.

10. The least likely place to find a reptile would be a
    - ❑ a. desert.
    - ❑ b. swamp.
    - ❑ c. mountaintop.

Poisonous Snakes of the United States

Poisonous snakes have glands that make poison, also called venom. Most poisonous snakes in the United States are pit vipers. These snakes have long, hollow fangs that push venom deep into the victim's flesh. Their bites are rarely fatal to humans. Pit vipers have pits, or dents, between the eyes and nostrils. The pits sense small changes in temperature and help the snakes find prey. Most pit vipers come out at night to hunt.

There are three kinds of pit vipers in the United States: copperheads, rattlesnakes, and cottonmouths. Copperheads get their name from their copper-colored heads and bodies. They live in swampy, forested, or rocky areas of the central and eastern parts of the country. Rattlesnakes have rattles on the ends of their tails. They shake them when threatened. Rattlesnakes are found in several parts of the country. Diamondback rattlesnakes are the most dangerous, because they can be quite large and sometimes aggressive. Cottonmouths are named for the white lining of their mouths. They live in southeastern swamps and are also called water moccasins. They are aggressive in protecting their territory, and they have strong venom.

Coral snakes are not pit vipers, but they have very strong venom. Fortunately, they are not aggressive. They are usually active at night and in the early morning. They are colored in bright bands of red, black, and yellow, and are found in the Southeast and Southwest.

1. **Recognizing Words in Context**

Find the word *aggressive* in the passage. One definition below is closest to the meaning of that word. One definition has the opposite or nearly opposite meaning. The remaining definition has a completely different meaning. Label the definitions C for *closest*, O for *opposite or nearly opposite*, and D for *different*.

_____ a. peaceful

_____ b. moving carefully

_____ c. likely to attack

2. **Distinguishing Fact from Opinion**

Two of the statements below present *facts*, which can be proved correct. The other statement is an *opinion*, which expresses someone's thoughts or beliefs. Label the statements F for *fact* and O for *opinion*.

_____ a. Diamondback rattlesnakes are more dangerous than coral snakes are.

_____ b. Cottonmouths are also called water moccasins.

_____ c. Coral snakes are not pit vipers.

3. Keeping Events in Order

Label the statements below 1, 2, and 3 to show the order in which the events happen.

_____ a. A person walks close to where a rattlesnake is resting.

_____ b. The rattlesnake strikes.

_____ c. The rattlesnake shakes its rattle.

4. Making Correct Inferences

Two of the statements below are correct *inferences,* or reasonable guesses. They are based on information in the passage. The other statement is an incorrect, or faulty, inference. Label the statements C for *correct* inference and F for *faulty* inference.

_____ a. Poisonous snakes live mainly in the warmer regions of the United States.

_____ b. Snakes that have pits in front of their eyes should be avoided.

_____ c. Coral snakes never bite people, because they are not aggressive.

5. Understanding Main Ideas

One of the statements below expresses the main idea of the passage. One statement is too general, or too broad. The other explains only part of the passage; it is too narrow. Label the statements M for *main idea,* B for *too broad,* and N for *too narrow.*

_____ a. Poisonous snakes that live in the United States are pit vipers and coral snakes.

_____ b. Coral snakes have strong venom.

_____ c. Snakes can be found in most parts of the world.

Correct Answers, Part A _____

Correct Answers, Part B _____

Total Correct Answers _____

Plants that grow flowers are called angiosperms. About 80 percent of all green plants are angiosperms. Angiosperms form the basis of food webs for animals that live on land. These plants also provide medicine, fibers, hardwood, and other valuable products. Flowering plants have four main parts: flowers, leaves, stems, and roots. Each part has an important purpose.

Flowers come in a variety of colors, shapes, and sizes. Their purpose is to produce seeds that can grow into new plants. Seeds are produced in the middle of flowers, in the carpels. Next to the carpels are the stamens. These are tall, thin structures that produce pollen. For seeds to grow, pollen from the stamens must enter the carpels. This process, called pollination, takes place when birds, insects, or the wind moves pollen from stamen to carpel within the same plant or from plant to plant. It is usually better for a flower to receive pollen from a separate plant. Surrounding the stamens are the petals. Petals give flowers their color and fragrance. The color and fragrance help attract insects and birds to the plants, increasing pollination.

Leaves make food for angiosperms. They do this through a process called photosynthesis. Leaf cells contain tiny structures called chloroplasts, which are full of green chlorophyll. The chloroplasts absorb energy from sunlight and turn it into food energy for the plant. Leaves also have pores called stomata that allow carbon dioxide in and oxygen out. If a plant takes in too much water, the plant can release it through the stomata. Leaves also store food and water. They come in many shapes and sizes.

Stems hold up the leaves and flowers. They also carry food and water to other parts of the plant. Stems have buds from which leaves and flowers grow. In some plants large buds called bulbs grow underground and provide food for a plant to survive the winter. Tulips and daffodils are examples of flowering plants with bulbs. The stems of flowering trees are made of wood and are called trunks.

A plant's roots keep the plant in place. They also absorb the water and minerals the plant needs to live. Almost all roots grow underground. Some angiosperms have a taproot, a thick main root that grows downward with smaller roots branching off it. Others have fibrous roots, which are thinner and spread out closer to the surface. These tiny hairlike roots help to absorb more water and minerals.

Reading Time _____

Recalling Facts

1. The four main parts of flowering plants are
   - ❏ a. flowers, leaves, stems, and roots.
   - ❏ b. flowers, leaves, buds, and petals.
   - ❏ c. flowers, stems, sepals, and carpels.

2. Flowering plants are also called
   - ❏ a. angioplasties.
   - ❏ b. gymnosperms.
   - ❏ c. angiosperms.

3. The purpose of a flower is to
   - ❏ a. protect the plant from being eaten.
   - ❏ b. support the plant.
   - ❏ c. produce seeds.

4. Stems
   - ❏ a. create food for plants.
   - ❏ b. carry food and water.
   - ❏ c. keep the plant in place.

5. A taproot is
   - ❏ a. a main root that grows downward.
   - ❏ b. thin and threadlike.
   - ❏ c. a bulb.

Understanding Ideas

6. From the information given in this article, one can conclude that
   - ❏ a. the flower is the most important part of a flowering plant.
   - ❏ b. the stem is not as important as the other parts of a plant.
   - ❏ c. all parts of the plant work together to help the plant survive.

7. From the article, one can infer that
   - ❏ a. pollen travels from flower to flower in several ways.
   - ❏ b. pollination could never take place without wind.
   - ❏ c. only insects can pollinate flowers.

8. One can infer that if all of the chloroplasts in a flowering plant were destroyed, the plant would
   - ❏ a. not be able to take in any water.
   - ❏ b. immediately shrivel up and die.
   - ❏ c. not be able to make its food.

9. One can infer that trees can survive without leaves in winter because
   - ❏ a. photosynthesis also takes place in the roots.
   - ❏ b. trees store food during the seasons when they have leaves.
   - ❏ c. trees hibernate during the winter.

10. If a potted flowering plant were kept inside a dark cupboard, it would probably die because
    - ❏ a. the roots could not grow.
    - ❏ b. photosynthesis could not take place.
    - ❏ c. there would be no insects or wind to spread pollen.

Animal Helpers in the Garden

Most gardeners think of insects and other animals as pests that destroy garden plants. It is true that many kinds of animals enjoy a tasty meal in gardens. But there are also animals that help keep gardens healthy.

Plants do not grow well in dense soil. They prefer soil that has space for oxygen to enter and water to drain away. Earthworm tunnels provide this kind of space. Garden soil also needs lots of organic matter. Organic matter comes from dead plants and animals and from animal waste. Earthworms take in organic matter and soil. They bring deep soil to the top in the form of casts, which are their wastes. The casts provide nutrients for garden plants. When earthworms die, they become organic matter themselves.

Aphids are tiny bugs that injure plants by sucking plant sap from stems. Ladybugs, also called ladybird beetles, eat aphids and other pests. Ladybugs can save plants and crops. Farmers and gardeners sometimes buy ladybugs and turn them loose on their plants.

In order for plants to grow fruit, vegetables, and seeds, they must be pollinated. Bees, butterflies, and hummingbirds help spread pollen when they take nectar from flowers. As they remove nectar, pollen rubs off on them and is carried from plant to plant.

1. **Recognizing Words in Context**

   Find the word *organic* in the passage. One definition below is closest to the meaning of that word. One definition has the opposite or nearly opposite meaning. The remaining definition has a completely different meaning. Label the definitions C for *closest*, O for *opposite or nearly opposite*, and D for *different*.

   _____ a. from sick plants

   _____ b. from nonliving things

   _____ c. from living things

2. **Distinguishing Fact from Opinion**

   Two of the statements below present *facts*, which can be proved correct. The other statement is an *opinion*, which expresses someone's thoughts or beliefs. Label the statements F for *fact* and O for *opinion*.

   _____ a. Earthworm tunnels help oxygen to get into soil.

   _____ b. Bees move pollen from plant to plant.

   _____ c. Buying ladybugs is the best way to get rid of aphids.

3. Keeping Events in Order

Label the statements below 1, 2, and 3 to show the order in which the events happen.

_____ a. The garden soil becomes less dense and richer in nutrients.

_____ b. A gardener buys a container of earthworms and spreads the worms around the garden.

_____ c. Earthworms dig tunnels in the garden.

4. Making Correct Inferences

Two of the statements below are correct *inferences,* or reasonable guesses. They are based on information in the passage. The other statement is an incorrect, or faulty, inference. Label the statements C for *correct* inference and F for *faulty* inference.

_____ a. Aphids will destroy all garden plants if there are few ladybugs around.

_____ b. Earthworms help improve garden soil in several ways.

_____ c. Farmers do not mind having bees in their fields.

5. Understanding Main Ideas

One of the statements below expresses the main idea of the passage. One statement is too general, or too broad. The other explains only part of the passage; it is too narrow. Label the statements M for *main idea*, B for *too broad*, and N for *too narrow*.

_____ a. Different kinds of animals can be found in gardens.

_____ b. Some animals can be helpful to gardeners.

_____ c. Ladybugs eat aphids.

Correct Answers, Part A _____

Correct Answers, Part B _____

Total Correct Answers _____

A baseball thrown to a batter and a leaf blown from a tree are two examples of how natural forces act on objects in the air. When an object is released in the air, it usually falls downward. To understand what happens to an object in the air, one needs to understand the concept of gravity and the effect of air resistance. On Earth, gravity can be thought of as a downward force. Air resistance is an upward force on a falling object. The combination of these two forces is what makes an object fall at a particular speed, or velocity.

Gravity, one of the most basic forces of nature, makes objects fall. Gravity is the force that pulls objects toward Earth. If a person lets go of two objects that are the same size, shape, and weight, they fall at the same speed.

Many people think of air as being weightless, but air is actually a gas that consists mainly of nitrogen and oxygen. Earth's atmosphere contains quadrillions of tons of air. Air resistance is the force of the air pushing against a moving object. Air resistance is also called drag. The amount of air resistance an object encounters when it falls depends primarily on its weight, size, and shape. For example, suppose a 6-kilogram (13-pound) sheet of plastic and a 6-kilogram bowling ball were dropped from the top of a tall building at the same time. The bowling ball would hit the ground long before the sheet of plastic would. The reason is that the plastic would encounter more air resistance on its way down. This is mainly because the plastic sheet has a much larger surface than the bowling ball does. More air would be pushing against the plastic than would be pushing against the bowling ball.

If two objects are the same shape and the same weight, their size will usually determine which falls faster. A 6-kilogram ball made of plastic is larger than a 6-kilogram ball made of steel. More air will push on the larger object, so the steel ball will fall faster.

A parachute takes advantage of air resistance to slow a person's fall. Even though a person weighs more wearing a parachute than without one, the parachute will still cause the person to fall more slowly. An open parachute creates a large surface area and much more air resistance.

Reading Time _____

Recalling Facts

1. The force that pulls objects toward Earth is called
   - ❏ a. speed.
   - ❏ b. gravity.
   - ❏ c. air resistance.

2. Air is made up of
   - ❏ a. nothing.
   - ❏ b. only oxygen atoms.
   - ❏ c. a gas.

3. The speed at which an object falls is determined mainly by the object's
   - ❏ a. shape, size, and magnetism.
   - ❏ b. shape, size, and weight.
   - ❏ c. shape, color, and weight.

4. The force that pushes against a falling object is called
   - ❏ a. gravity.
   - ❏ b. levity.
   - ❏ c. air resistance.

5. Parachutes work by increasing
   - ❏ a. air resistance.
   - ❏ b. gravity.
   - ❏ c. weight.

Understanding Ideas

6. One can infer that the reason a leaf falls slowly from a tree is that a leaf has
   - ❏ a. resistance to gravity.
   - ❏ b. a large surface area for an object of its weight.
   - ❏ c. magnetic attraction to a tree.

7. If an oak board and an oak cube of the same weight were dropped from the top of a building at the same time, which would hit the ground first?
   - ❏ a. The board would.
   - ❏ b. The cube would.
   - ❏ c. They would hit at the same time.

8. If the speed of an object increases as it falls, then an object dropped from a higher distance has a final speed that is _____ an object dropped from a lower distance.
   - ❏ a. slower than
   - ❏ b. faster than
   - ❏ c. the same as

9. It is likely that a strong wind causes objects to fall
   - ❏ a. faster.
   - ❏ b. at the same speed as they would otherwise.
   - ❏ c. more slowly.

10. One can infer that without air resistance, all objects would fall
    - ❏ a. slowly.
    - ❏ b. at speeds much different from one another.
    - ❏ c. at about the same speed as one another.

Streamlined Trains

Modern trains come in a variety of shapes and sizes. In one way, however, they are similar. Almost all of them are designed to be highly streamlined. When engineers streamline machines, they shape them so that air resistance is minimized.

Trains have not always been streamlined. In the 19th century, trains had flat fronts and were bulky. For example, many trains were powered by steam locomotives that had large water tanks shaped like cylinders and smokestacks that stuck up in the air. The round sides of the water tanks faced forward and created a lot of air resistance.

Air resistance was not a big problem at first because it has a great effect only on trains that travel at high speed. In the 1960s Japan developed an electric train that could travel faster than 300 kilometers per hour (186 miles per hour). The development of electric locomotives had eliminated the need for tanks and smokestacks. The high-speed Japanese train was called a bullet train because the front of the train had a streamlined shape that looked somewhat like a bullet.

Streamlined designs improved trains in two ways. They increased speed and reduced the amount of energy needed to power the trains. Streamlined designs are also important in other forms of transportation, especially airplanes.

1. Recognizing Words in Context

Find the word *minimized* in the passage. One definition below is closest to the meaning of that word. One definition has the opposite or nearly opposite meaning. The remaining definition has a completely different meaning. Label the definitions C for *closest*, O for *opposite or nearly opposite*, and D for *different*.

_____ a. decreased as much as possible

_____ b. kept at the same level

_____ c. increased as much as possible

2. Distinguishing Fact from Opinion

Two of the statements below present *facts*, which can be proved correct. The other statement is an *opinion*, which expresses someone's thoughts or beliefs. Label the statements F for *fact* and O for *opinion*.

_____ a. Streamlined trains use less energy than ones with flat fronts.

_____ b. Steam locomotives encountered a lot of air resistance.

_____ c. One of the best ways to travel is on a streamlined train.

3. Keeping Events in Order

Label the statements below 1, 2, and 3 to show the order in which the events happened.

_____ a. The first electric locomotive was built.

_____ b. The first steam locomotive was built.

_____ c. The first bullet train was built.

4. Making Correct Inferences

Two of the statements below are correct *inferences,* or reasonable guesses. They are based on information in the passage. The other statement is an incorrect, or faulty, inference. Label the statements C for *correct* inference and F for *faulty* inference.

_____ a. Cars that have streamlined designs are likely to use less gas than cars that are the same size and do not have streamlined designs.

_____ b. If steam locomotives had been streamlined, they would not have gone much faster.

_____ c. Steam locomotives were more expensive to operate than bullet trains are.

5. Understanding Main Ideas

One of the statements below expresses the main idea of the passage. One statement is too general, or too broad. The other explains only part of the passage; it is too narrow. Label the statements M for *main idea,* B for *too broad,* and N for *too narrow.*

_____ a. The design of machines used for transportation has improved.

_____ b. Streamlined designs have allowed trains to go faster and use less energy.

_____ c. Steam locomotives had water tanks that were shaped like cylinders.

Correct Answers, Part A _____

Correct Answers, Part B _____

Total Correct Answers _____

Spiders belong to a group of animals called arachnids. Scientists do not consider spiders to be insects because spiders have eight legs and two-part bodies. Insects have six legs and three-part bodies. Insects are the favorite food of most spiders. Many spiders use a sticky, silky material to spin webs that trap insects. The silk comes from small limbs, called spinnerets, on the spider's belly.

The wolf spider is a common type of spider. Most wolf spiders have long legs and bodies that stay close to the ground. They do not trap their prey in webs. Instead, they grab it with their front legs and crush it with their jaws. One kind of wolf spider is the trap-door spider. This spider lives in a burrow covered by a trapdoor made from silk and dirt. It flips open the trapdoor and grabs its prey by surprise as the prey walks by. Another type of wolf spider is the tarantula, which is known for its large, hairy body.

Many people are afraid of spiders. Although all spiders are poisonous, their bites are rarely fatal. Small children and senior citizens are most at risk. In the United States the spiders with the most dangerous poisons are the black widow and the brown recluse. Among black widows, only adult females are dangerous. They are about 4 centimeters ($1^1/2$ inches) long and have a reddish hourglass mark on their black bodies. Black widows prefer to build webs outside in dark places close to the ground—for example, in a woodpile or at the base of a shed. Like most other spiders, black widows are not aggressive and usually bite only when disturbed.

The brown recluse spider is a small brown spider with long legs. It is found mainly in Southern states. It prefers quiet areas near the ground—for example, in the corner of a closet floor. It may hide in fabrics if they are not used for long periods of time. This spider is also called the violin spider because of a dark, violin-shaped mark behind its eyes.

Funnel-web spiders are small with brownish-gray bodies. They build webs with a funnel back, where the spider rests. In front of the funnel is a sheet web that traps insects. The spider feels vibrations on the web, goes to the insect, and bites it. It wraps its prey in silk and drags it into the funnel.

Reading Time _____

Recalling Facts

1. Spiders are
   - ❑ a. crustaceans.
   - ❑ b. insects.
   - ❑ c. arachnids.

2. The trap-door spider is one kind of
   - ❑ a. wolf spider.
   - ❑ b. funnel-web spider.
   - ❑ c. brown recluse spider.

3. One of the most poisonous spiders is the
   - ❑ a. trap-door spider.
   - ❑ b. funnel-web spider.
   - ❑ c. brown recluse spider.

4. A female adult black widow spider has a mark on it that looks like a
   - ❑ a. black violin.
   - ❑ b. red hourglass.
   - ❑ c. yellow egg.

5. Spiders have _____ legs.
   - ❑ a. four
   - ❑ b. eight
   - ❑ c. twelve

Understanding Ideas

6. One can conclude from reading this article that spiders help people by
   - ❑ a. rarely going inside homes.
   - ❑ b. keeping the insect population under control.
   - ❑ c. eliminating most mosquitoes.

7. A person who lives in the South and finds some dusty old clothes in an unused closet should watch out for a _____ spider.
   - ❑ a. brown recluse
   - ❑ b. wolf
   - ❑ c. black widow

8. You can infer that if you notice a black widow spider in a web on the outside of your house, you should
   - ❑ a. stay away from it and notify an adult.
   - ❑ b. try to kill it immediately.
   - ❑ c. find some matches and burn it up.

9. From the facts presented in this article, one can conclude that
   - ❑ a. all spiders jump on their prey.
   - ❑ b. spiders catch prey in different ways.
   - ❑ c. all spiders spin webs to catch their prey.

10. The best way to tell one kind of spider from another is by
    - ❑ a. the number of legs each has.
    - ❑ b. their sizes and markings.
    - ❑ c. the type of web each one spins.

Dr. Charles Turner, Zoologist

Zoologists are scientists who study animals. One zoologist who learned a lot about spiders and insects was Dr. Charles Turner.

Turner was born in Ohio in 1867. He was the son of slaves who were freed after the Civil War. As a young boy, Turner wanted to know about insects. He would sit and observe bees, ants, and other bugs for hours. He wanted to know why they acted the way they did. He asked his teachers lots of questions about insects. One of them told Turner to find out for himself.

So that's what he did. He went to school and earned a master's degree from the University of Cincinnati. Then he taught biology at a college for several years. In 1907, he earned a doctorate from the University of Chicago. He then taught high school instead of college because it gave him more time to study insects.

Turner was one of the first scientists to show that insects can hear, and he also showed that they could distinguish between pitches. He showed that cockroaches can learn. He sent the roaches through a maze again and again, and they learned to avoid dead ends. Turner became a leading authority on the behavior of ants and spiders. He published a number of books about insects.

1. **Recognizing Words in Context**

   Find the word *distinguish* in the passage. One definition below is closest to the meaning of that word. One definition has the opposite or nearly opposite meaning. The remaining definition has a completely different meaning. Label the definitions C for *closest*, O for *opposite or nearly opposite*, and D for *different*.

   _____ a. misunderstand

   _____ b. recognize

   _____ c. extinguish

2. **Distinguishing Fact from Opinion**

   Two of the statements below present *facts*, which can be proved correct. The other statement is an *opinion*, which expresses someone's thoughts or beliefs. Label the statements F for *fact* and O for *opinion*.

   _____ a. Insects can hear.

   _____ b. The study of insects is one of the most important areas of science.

   _____ c. Charles Turner was a zoologist.

3. **Keeping Events in Order**

   Label the statements below 1, 2, and 3 to show the order in which the events happened.

   _____ a. Turner taught biology at a college.

   _____ b. Turner earned a master's degree.

   _____ c. Turner taught high school.

4. **Making Correct Inferences**

   Two of the statements below are correct *inferences,* or reasonable guesses. They are based on information in the passage. The other statement is an incorrect, or faulty, inference. Label the statements C for *correct* inference and F for *faulty* inference.

   _____ a. Some zoologists study insects.

   _____ b. Turner was one of the first Americans to study zoology.

   _____ c. Cockroaches are not the only insects that are capable of learning.

5. **Understanding Main Ideas**

   One of the statements below expresses the main idea of the passage. One statement is too general, or too broad. The other explains only part of the passage; it is too narrow. Label the statements M for *main idea,* B for *too broad,* and N for *too narrow.*

   _____ a. Charles Turner was a zoologist who made important discoveries about insects.

   _____ b. Zoology is a branch of science.

   _____ c. Charles Turner proved that insects could hear.

Correct Answers, Part A _____

Correct Answers, Part B _____

Total Correct Answers _____

A habitat is a place where certain kinds of plants and animals normally live. A pond is one kind of habitat.

A type of plant that often grows in the shallow water at the edge of a pond is the cattail. Cattails are tall green reeds that have cylinder-shaped brown tops with a velvetlike surface. Groups of cattails provide excellent nesting areas for birds, muskrats, and other pond animals. Cattails are also a source of food for these animals.

The surface of a pond may have areas of floating green scum. Pond scum is made up of tiny plants called algae. Algae may also grow on rocks below the water's surface. Algae serve as food for many animals, including protozoa, which are too small to be seen without a microscope.

Another type of plant found in some ponds is the water lily. Water lilies have large, round leaves that float. Each leaf is attached to a stem that stretches all the way to the muddy bottom. These floating plants provide homes for beetles, dragonfly larvae, and snails.

The still waters of a pond are a good place for female mosquitoes to lay their eggs. The eggs hatch into larvae. The larvae move through the water by wriggling. Although some of these larvae will live to become adult mosquitoes, many of them will end up as food for fish.

Ducks are one group of pond animals that eat mosquito larvae; they also eat other insects and plants. Mallard ducks can often be seen swimming in ponds. The males have white bellies and brownish chests. Their heads and throats are dark green, and they have a white band around their necks. The females are nearly solid brown, with darker brown spots and markings.

Fish, too, are found in ponds. Pond fish include bream, crappies, and bass. They feed on larvae, snails, adult insects, and worms.

Ponds are favorite habitats for frogs. Female frogs like to lay their eggs in still water. The many insects that live in and around ponds provide frogs with food. Frogs are cold-blooded, and so when the temperature becomes uncomfortably warm or cold, frogs may bury themselves in the mud at the edges of ponds.

Egrets and heron are two kinds of large birds that hunt pond fish. These birds wade in the water on long legs and use their sharp bills to catch the fish.

Reading Time _____

Recalling Facts

1. Pond scum is made up of tiny plants called
   - ❑ a. larvae.
   - ❑ b. algae.
   - ❑ c. cattails.

2. Water lilies have
   - ❑ a. small oval leaves.
   - ❑ b. white petals and yellow centers.
   - ❑ c. stems that reach down to the bottom of a pond.

3. According to the article, two kinds of large birds that sometimes hunt in ponds are
   - ❑ a. egrets and herons.
   - ❑ b. gulls and vultures.
   - ❑ c. sandpipers and egrets.

4. _____ can often be found in groups of cattails.
   - ❑ a. Beaver dams
   - ❑ b. Buried frogs
   - ❑ c. Bird nests

5. Mosquito larvae are eaten by
   - ❑ a. fish.
   - ❑ b. muskrats.
   - ❑ c. flies.

Understanding Ideas

6. From the information in the article, one can conclude that
   - ❑ a. a pond provides food and shelter for many kinds of animals.
   - ❑ b. all pond animals eat insects or other animals.
   - ❑ c. all pond animals live underwater.

7. A person would be unlikely to find frogs living in a pond
   - ❑ a. on a large island.
   - ❑ b. in a valley.
   - ❑ c. in the mountains.

8. If mosquitoes laid a large number of eggs on a pond, what could a person do to prevent a massive hatching of mosquitoes?
   - ❑ a. try to train frogs to eat the eggs
   - ❑ b. make sure the pond had a healthy population of fish
   - ❑ c. add algae to the pond

9. One can infer that most ponds have balanced populations of animals because
   - ❑ a. almost all of the animals serve as food for other animals.
   - ❑ b. if the population of one type of animal gets too large, the group moves to another pond.
   - ❑ c. people carefully control the animal populations of ponds.

10. In order for animals to thrive in a pond,
    - ❑ a. water must be in constant motion.
    - ❑ b. a forest must be nearby.
    - ❑ c. plant life is essential.

What Is an Ecosystem?

As Ms. Kane's science class was preparing to go on a field trip to a forest, Ms. Kane said that all the plants and animals that live in a particular type of area, together with their surroundings, make up an *ecosystem.*

In the forest, Nam found three living things: a squirrel, birds, and an oak tree. Then Eva saw mushrooms and a mosquito.

Fred scooped up some dirt. "The soil is part of the surroundings," he said, "and so are the air and the amount of rain and the temperature."

"Right," Ms. Kane said. "These are all part of this forest ecosystem. Another important fact about ecosystems is that all the living things depend on one another. The oak tree is a home for the birds and the squirrels. Acorns that fall from the tree are food for the squirrels. The squirrels carry some of the acorns away, and so oak trees will sprout somewhere else." Then Eva brought up how insects carry pollen from flower to flower. Nam added that birds eat insects.

"All living things in an ecosystem depend on the environment," Ms. Kane said. "The tree needs the soil and the rain to grow. Animals need water to drink." Then Ms. Kane asked the students to think of other ecosystems.

The students came up with a desert, a prairie, a swamp, and the sea. Each is a distinct environment with its own combination of plants and animals.

1. **Recognizing Words in Context**

   Find the word *distinct* in the passage. One definition below is closest to the meaning of that word. One definition has the opposite or nearly opposite meaning. The remaining definition has a completely different meaning. Label the definitions C for *closest,* O for *opposite or nearly opposite,* and D for *different.*

   _____ a. the same as others

   _____ b. not like others

   _____ c. not natural

2. **Distinguishing Fact from Opinion**

   Two of the statements below present *facts,* which can be proved correct. The other statement is an *opinion,* which expresses someone's thoughts or beliefs. Label the statements F for *fact* and O for *opinion.*

   _____ a. A forest is a more important ecosystem than a prairie is.

   _____ b. A swamp is an ecosystem.

   _____ c. Living things depend on the environment.

3. **Keeping Events in Order**

Label the statements below 1, 2, and 3 to show the order in which the events happened.

_____ a. Ms. Kane defined the word *ecosystem*.

_____ b. The class thought of some other ecosystems.

_____ c. The class left on a field trip.

4. **Making Correct Inferences**

Two of the statements below are correct *inferences*, or reasonable guesses. They are based on information in the passage. The other statement is an incorrect, or faulty, inference. Label the statements C for *correct* inference and F for *faulty* inference.

_____ a. In an ecosystem, there is always one part that is much more important than the others.

_____ b. The entire Earth is an ecosystem.

_____ c. A pond is an ecosystem.

5. **Understanding Main Ideas**

One of the statements below expresses the main idea of the passage. One statement is too general, or too broad. The other explains only part of the passage; it is too narrow. Label the statements M for *main idea*, B for *too broad*, and N for *too narrow*.

_____ a. In an ecosystem, living things depend on one another and on the environment.

_____ b. There are many types of plants and animals on Earth.

_____ c. Squirrels depend on trees for shelter and food.

Correct Answers, Part A _____

Correct Answers, Part B _____

Total Correct Answers _____

Memory plays a key role in the workings of a computer. Computer programs cannot be run without memory. Memory also allows files to be saved and used again. Many types of memory are used in these and other tasks. All types can be grouped into two main forms. These forms are short-term memory and permanent storage.

When a person turns on a computer, the computer loads data from permanent storage into short-term memory. It also loads data in this way when a program or file is opened. The basic programs the computer needs to begin working are stored in a type of permanent storage called ROM. ROM stands for "Read-Only Memory." The data stored here can be read but not changed. Most programs, and files that can be changed as well as read, are stored on hard drives or diskettes. All forms of permanent storage hold data even when the computer is turned off.

When a file is in use, the computer loads data from storage to short-term memory called RAM, or Random Access Memory. Unlike ROM, RAM does not hold data when the power is switched off. That is why a change made to a file should be saved to the hard drive or to a diskette. RAM is important because it makes tasks much faster. It allows the central processing unit of the computer to access and use data at high speeds. The central processing unit, or CPU, directs the operations of a computer.

One way to think of the relationship between permanent storage and RAM is to picture a shelf full of books and a desk. A person who needs information moves certain books from the shelf to the desk. Once they are on the desk, the books can be left open to the important pages. The person can simply glance at the books and get the information. Just as the desk full of books provides quick access to data, so does RAM.

A second type of short-term memory is Static Random Access Memory, or SRAM. It is held in what is called a cache. The data that is used the most is held in a cache in the CPU. This allows access to the most important data at the highest speeds. It cuts out the time it would take for this data to reach the CPU from RAM. Like RAM, a cache cannot hold data once power is switched off.

Reading Time _____

Recalling Facts

1. The two main forms of computer memory are
   - ❏ a. RAM and SRAM.
   - ❏ b. short-term memory and permanent storage.
   - ❏ c. ROM and hard drives.

2. When a file is in use, its data is loaded into
   - ❏ a. ROM.
   - ❏ b. RAM.
   - ❏ c. permanent storage.

3. A type of memory that stores data even when the power is switched off is
   - ❏ a. RAM.
   - ❏ b. SRAM.
   - ❏ c. ROM.

4. Because of RAM, tasks on a computer are
   - ❏ a. faster.
   - ❏ b. more complicated.
   - ❏ c. more secure.

5. A type of short-term memory called SRAM is held in
   - ❏ a. the hard drive.
   - ❏ b. permanent storage.
   - ❏ c. the central processing unit.

Understanding Ideas

6. The article suggests that the main purpose of ROM is allowing the computer to
   - ❏ a. start up and run.
   - ❏ b. open more files.
   - ❏ c. perform tasks instantly.

7. Unlike the short-term memory SRAM, RAM
   - ❏ a. does not hold only data that are in use.
   - ❏ b. decreases computer speed.
   - ❏ c. is not held in the central processing unit.

8. Once saved, changes made to a computer file would most likely be stored
   - ❏ a. on the hard drive.
   - ❏ b. in RAM.
   - ❏ c. in ROM.

9. If a computer were running very slowly, it could be assumed that
   - ❏ a. any diskettes being used were full.
   - ❏ b. there was not enough RAM available.
   - ❏ c. the CPU was not very good.

10. If a person bought a new software program and installed it in a computer, the program would be stored
    - ❏ a. in RAM.
    - ❏ b. on the hard drive.
    - ❏ c. in the CPU.

From Punch Cards to DVDs

People have been storing computer data on removable devices ever since computers were invented. Some of the first computers punched out holes on paper cards to store data. Magnetic tape—such as that used in cassettes—was another early form of storage device.

Today, removable storage takes many forms. Diskettes are an economical, easy-to-use form of storage. Although storage space on a diskette is small, newer diskettes called removable storage disks hold much more data. Compact discs, or CDs, that could once only be read by a computer can now be used for storage. Data are changed into patterns of light created by a laser. The patterns are recorded on filmlike material bonded to a CD. CDs and digital video discs, or DVDs, can store many times the amount of data held on removable storage disks. The only device that can store more data is a removable hard drive, often called a platter. This type of storage is like a second hard drive. It can store as much as a built-in hard drive and works just as fast.

Removable storage devices have many important uses. The devices can be used to carry data from place to place. People use them to make "back-up" copies of data so that if a hard drive is damaged data will not be lost. Removable storage devices are also used to free up storage space on the computer.

1. Recognizing Words in Context

Find the word *economical* in the passage. One definition below is closest to the meaning of that word. One definition has the opposite or nearly opposite meaning. The remaining definition has a completely different meaning. Label the definitions C for *closest*, O for *opposite or nearly opposite*, and D for *different*.

_____ a. inexpensive

_____ b. expensive

_____ c. excellent

2. Distinguishing Fact from Opinion

Two of the statements below present *facts*, which can be proved correct. The other statement is an *opinion*, which expresses someone's thoughts or beliefs. Label the statements F for *fact* and O for *opinion*.

_____ a. A recordable CD can store more data than a diskette can.

_____ b. A DVD is the best option for removable data storage.

_____ c. Paper punch cards were once used to store data.

3. Keeping Events in Order

Label the statements below 1, 2, and 3 to show the order in which the events happened.

_____ a. Removable storage disks were invented.

_____ b. Diskettes were invented.

_____ c. Paper punch cards were invented.

4. Making Correct Inferences

Two of the statements below are correct *inferences,* or reasonable guesses. They are based on information in the passage. The other statement is an incorrect, or faulty, inference. Label the statements C for *correct* inference and F for *faulty* inference.

_____ a. DVDs will remain popular for decades.

_____ b. Diskettes are not as popular as they used to be.

_____ c. A removable hard drive has far more storage space than a removable storage disk.

5. Understanding Main Ideas

One of the statements below expresses the main idea of the passage. One statement is too general, or too broad. The other explains only part of the passage; it is too narrow. Label the statements M for *main idea,* B for *too broad,* and N for *too narrow.*

_____ a. Computer data can be stored either inside or outside the computer.

_____ b. Removable storage devices have improved over the years.

_____ c. Magnetic tape was an early type of removable storage device.

Correct Answers, Part A _____

Correct Answers, Part B _____

Total Correct Answers _____

The equator divides the world into the Northern Hemisphere and the Southern Hemisphere. The United States lies in the Northern Hemisphere. In the Northern Hemisphere, spring begins in late March and lasts until late June.

Although people may say that spring starts on a particular day, changes in the weather do not happen all at once. They happen gradually as Earth revolves. The tilt of Earth brings the Northern Hemisphere closer to the Sun. This causes the weather slowly to warm. People notice the Sun rising earlier and setting later each day.

There are differences in the signs of spring across the United States. Early signs of spring in colder regions, such as the Northeast, can be seen on the ground and in plant and animal life. One early sign of spring in these regions is the "ice-out." This is when the ice melts on rivers, lakes, and ponds.

Another early sign of spring is the blooming of a small white flower called a snowdrop. Snowdrops grow from underground buds called bulbs. In a sunny patch of ground, snowdrops can bloom as early as February. More spring flowers soon follow. One early flower that can bloom in March is the crocus. The appearance of crocuses is followed by those of daffodils and tulips.

In the woods, ferns start to push up through the soil and tree buds begin to form. Then comes "leaf-out." This is when the new leaves emerge from the buds.

Earthworm migration, or movement, is another sign of spring. As the ground warms and thaws, earthworms move about a meter (3.3 feet) closer to the surface. This migration happens when the temperature of the ground is about 2 degrees Celsius (36 degrees Fahrenheit).

As the earthworms appear, the robins come back from the south. A robin, with its red or orange feathers, pulling up an earthworm is a sure sign of spring. Another bird that arrives in the spring is the red-winged blackbird. The male is black with a red bar on its wings. Males arrive in the North before the females and sing to mark their territories. Groups of males can be seen in marshy areas and around lakes in the early spring.

A sound of spring is the croaking of spring peepers. These small brown frogs live along the edges of woods and wet areas. Their croaks sound like whistles and can be heard from far away.

Reading Time _____

Recalling Facts

1. In the Northern Hemisphere, spring begins in
   - ❏ a. late January.
   - ❏ b. mid-February.
   - ❏ c. late March.

2. The climate change from winter to spring
   - ❏ a. happens in stages.
   - ❏ b. occurs on a certain date.
   - ❏ c. happens suddenly.

3. "Ice-out"
   - ❏ a. is another name for a snowdrop.
   - ❏ b. is the melting of the ice on rivers, lakes, and ponds.
   - ❏ c. always happens in February.

4. Earthworm migration
   - ❏ a. happens when the ground warms and thaws.
   - ❏ b. is a result of "ice-out."
   - ❏ c. happens in the winter.

5. A spring peeper is
   - ❏ a. a small brown frog.
   - ❏ b. a black bird with a red bar on its wing.
   - ❏ c. an earthworm.

Understanding Ideas

6. One can conclude from reading this article that
   - ❏ a. spring arrives on a different day each year.
   - ❏ b. there are many signs of spring's arrival.
   - ❏ c. during spring, days are shorter than they are in the winter.

7. If a person sees a group of daffodils starting to bloom, it is most likely
   - ❏ a. January or February.
   - ❏ b. March or April.
   - ❏ c. May or June.

8. One can infer that during winter the tilt of Earth causes the Northern Hemisphere to be _____ the Sun.
   - ❏ a. closer to
   - ❏ b. farther from
   - ❏ c. hidden from

9. One can infer that in the Southern Hemisphere spring
   - ❏ a. is the warmest time of the year.
   - ❏ b. always comes before winter.
   - ❏ c. does not begin in March.

10. Which of the following is *not* a sign of spring in the northeastern part of the United States?
    - ❏ a. Trees are fully covered with leaves.
    - ❏ b. A robin pulls a worm from the ground next to a crocus.
    - ❏ c. Peepers start croaking.

On August 15, Joseph started a nature journal. He wanted to write down the changes he observed as fall and winter approached. He wrote, "Today was hot and sunny. The baby robins are out of the nest. They follow their parents and beg for the worms that the parents find. The babies have speckled chests, and the adults' chests are solid red. The bees were collecting nectar from the tall hollyhocks. Three hummingbirds came to the feeder. It got dark tonight at nine o'clock. There were many fireflies."

Two weeks later, on September 1, Joseph wrote, "The robins were pulling out worms this morning. I can't tell the baby birds from the grownups. The bees have moved to the hosta plants, which now have blue flowers. Five hummingbirds came to the feeder. Darkness came at eight-thirty. There were only a few fireflies."

Joseph did not write again until October 10, when he observed, "It was cool today. The leaves are turning yellow, orange, and red, and the flowers are nothing but desiccated stalks. I saw a few bees and no hummingbirds. It got dark at eight o'clock."

Finally, on November 1, Joseph wrote, "It was cold today, and most of the leaves have fallen off the trees. I saw squirrels collecting nuts and a group of Canada geese flying south. It was dark by seven. Winter is on its way."

1. **Recognizing Words in Context**

   Find the word *desiccated* in the passage. One definition below is closest to the meaning of that word. One definition has the opposite or nearly opposite meaning. The remaining definition has a completely different meaning. Label the definitions C for *closest*, O for *opposite or nearly opposite*, and D for *different*.

   _____ a. colorful

   _____ b. dry

   _____ c. moist

2. **Distinguishing Fact from Opinion**

   Two of the statements below present *facts*, which can be proved correct. The other statement is an *opinion*, which expresses someone's thoughts or beliefs. Label the statements F for *fact* and O for *opinion*.

   _____ a. Joseph should have recorded more facts in his journal.

   _____ b. Young robins have speckled chests.

   _____ c. Sometimes Joseph saw bees collecting nectar.

3. Keeping Events in Order

Label the statements below 1, 2, and 3 to show the order in which the events happened.

_____ a. Joseph saw a few fireflies.

_____ b. Joseph saw many fireflies.

_____ c. Joseph saw that most of the leaves had fallen.

4. Making Correct Inferences

Two of the statements below are correct *inferences,* or reasonable guesses. They are based on information in the passage. The other statement is an incorrect, or faulty, inference. Label the statements C for *correct* inference and F for *faulty* inference.

_____ a. There are more hours of daylight in fall than there are in summer.

_____ b. Squirrels store food for the winter.

_____ c. During warmer months, Canada geese live in northern areas.

5. Understanding Main Ideas

One of the statements below expresses the main idea of the passage. One statement is too general, or too broad. The other explains only part of the passage; it is too narrow. Label the statements M for *main idea,* B for *too broad,* and N for *too narrow.*

_____ a. Joseph wrote in his journal about the changes he saw in nature.

_____ b. A nature journal can help a person learn about biology.

_____ c. Joseph wrote that he saw hummingbirds.

Correct Answers, Part A _____

Correct Answers, Part B _____

Total Correct Answers _____

Stone, Brick, and Concrete

Many modern building materials were first used in ancient times. Stone, brick, and concrete have been used in building for thousands of years. Until recent times, the ways in which people got and made these materials changed little.

More than 4,000 years ago, ancient Egyptians built great pyramids with huge blocks of stone. There were large deposits of limestone in Egypt. To break off slabs of stone from the deposits, workers used copper tools and wooden wedges. First they carved grooves in the stone with their tools. Then they put wedges into the grooves and soaked the wedges with water. Water causes wood to expand, so the wedges made the rock split into slabs. The workers moved the slabs to building sites using sleds, rafts, and ramps. This process changed little until the 17th century, when gunpowder was first used to split stone from deposits. In recent times, drills powered by motors have made the job much easier.

The first bricks were sun-dried mud bricks made in the ancient Middle East more than 6,000 years ago. To make the bricks, workers poured mud into molds and baked them in the sun. Fired bricks began to be widely used during the Roman Empire. The Romans baked, or fired, these clay bricks in ovens called kilns to make them strong. Firing bricks made them waterproof, too. The Romans cemented bricks together with a strong mortar made from limestone and volcanic ash. Today, bricks are produced in large plants with the aid of machines.

The ancient Romans developed the cement they used as mortar into the first concrete. They mixed volcanic ash with powdered limestone and crushed stone. Building was faster and easier than ever with the use of concrete. Instead of laying brick walls, the Romans built wooden frames that they filled with concrete. Once the poured concrete walls were dry, the wooden forms were torn down. With concrete, new structures such as domes could be built.

Concrete changed little until the 19th century. Then people developed stronger concrete by experimenting with different mixes of materials. They also began using iron together with concrete. Supporting concrete with iron beams proved to be a very strong building method. As steel began to replace iron, it was possible to build skyscrapers for the first time. Engineers have combined ancient building materials with modern ones to create stronger structures than ever before.

Reading Time _____

Recalling Facts

1. Stone, brick, and concrete were building materials first used in
   - ❑ a. ancient times.
   - ❑ b. the 17th century.
   - ❑ c. the 19th century.

2. To make the great pyramids of Egypt, workers cut stone with
   - ❑ a. motor-powered drills.
   - ❑ b. gunpowder.
   - ❑ c. copper tools and wedges of wood.

3. The first bricks were made
   - ❑ a. of sun-dried mud.
   - ❑ b. of fired clay.
   - ❑ c. in large plants with machines.

4. The Romans were able to build strong buildings quickly when they began using
   - ❑ a. iron.
   - ❑ b. concrete.
   - ❑ c. limestone.

5. Skyscrapers arose as a result of new uses of
   - ❑ a. mortar and brick.
   - ❑ b. concrete and steel.
   - ❑ c. stone and cement.

Understanding Ideas

6. The article suggests that stone, brick, and concrete have been used
   - ❑ a. in both ancient and modern times.
   - ❑ b. mostly by people in Europe.
   - ❑ c. only since the oven was invented.

7. One can infer that one of the reasons the Egyptian pyramids are still standing today is that
   - ❑ a. the ghosts of pharaohs have protected the pyramids.
   - ❑ b. the Egyptian government has rebuilt the pyramids several times.
   - ❑ c. the Egyptians used strong building materials and good construction methods.

8. It is likely that firing bricks makes them stronger because heat
   - ❑ a. melts some minerals into iron.
   - ❑ b. changes the clay into concrete.
   - ❑ c. causes chemical changes in the clay.

9. Why might motor-powered drills have replaced gunpowder as a way of breaking up rock?
   - ❑ a. Drills are more exact and less dangerous.
   - ❑ b. Gunpowder became very expensive to buy.
   - ❑ c. The supply of gunpowder ran out.

10. From the article, one can infer that the strongest buildings in use today
    - ❑ a. are made from a combination of building materials.
    - ❑ b. are made completely of steel.
    - ❑ c. are made of brick.

Some of the longest bridges in the world are suspension bridges. The deck, or flat part, of a suspension bridge hangs from two steel cables that stretch between tall towers. The towers extend deep into a layer of rock. They can support the bridge because of this firm base.

The Brooklyn Bridge is a suspension bridge in New York City that spans the East River to link Manhattan and Brooklyn. The building of this bridge was a major accomplishment because few structures that large had ever been built. It was finished in 1883, after 14 years of construction. Several workers lost their lives during the long and difficult project.

The soundness of the Brooklyn Bridge depended on firmly anchored towers and strong steel cables. Engineers created air-filled chambers on the floor of the river so that workers could make holes in which to place the towers. They dug deep into the riverbed until they reached a deep layer of rock that could anchor the towers. Once the towers and other supports were built, work began on the cables. Hundreds of steel wires were bound into many strands. Then the strands were spun into two large cables. Finally, the deck of the bridge was hung from the two large cables by attaching it with many smaller cables. At the time of its completion, the Brooklyn Bridge was the longest and tallest bridge ever built.

1. Recognizing Words in Context

Find the word *soundness* in the passage. One definition below is closest to the meaning of that word. One definition has the opposite or nearly opposite meaning. The remaining definition has a completely different meaning. Label the definitions C for *closest*, O for *opposite or nearly opposite*, and D for *different*.

_____ a. weakness

_____ b. volume

_____ c. reliability

2. Distinguishing Fact from Opinion

Two of the statements below present *facts*, which can be proved correct. The other statement is an *opinion*, which expresses someone's thoughts or beliefs. Label the statements F for *fact* and O for *opinion*.

_____ a. The Brooklyn Bridge took 14 years to build.

_____ b. The Brooklyn Bridge was a great achievement in engineering.

_____ c. Suspension bridges can be built across rivers.

3. **Keeping Events in Order**

Label the statements below 1, 2, and 3 to show the order in which the events happened.

_____ a. Strands of steel wire were made into two large cables.

_____ b. Workers dug holes in the riverbed.

_____ c. The deck of the bridge was connected to the large cables.

4. **Making Correct Inferences**

Two of the statements below are correct *inferences,* or reasonable guesses. They are based on information in the passage. The other statement is an incorrect, or faulty, inference. Label the statements C for *correct* inference and F for *faulty* inference.

_____ a. Building a large bridge requires many skilled workers.

_____ b. Some of the construction work on the Brooklyn Bridge was dangerous.

_____ c. The Brooklyn Bridge is still the longest bridge in the world.

5. **Understanding Main Ideas**

One of the statements below expresses the main idea of the passage. One statement is too general, or too broad. The other explains only part of the passage; it is too narrow. Label the statements M for *main idea,* B for *too broad,* and N for *too narrow.*

_____ a. The Brooklyn Bridge connects Brooklyn and Manhattan.

_____ b. Suspension bridges can be built across wide rivers.

_____ c. The Brooklyn Bridge was a major construction project in the late 1800s.

Correct Answers, Part A _____

Correct Answers, Part B _____

Total Correct Answers _____

The Tropical Rainforest Biome

A biome is a community of living things in a particular area. A tropical rain forest is one kind of biome. Most tropical rain forests are found near the equator, where it is hot and humid. Rain forest plants grow to many different heights, and so activity at the bottom layer of the rain forest is very different from what goes on at the top. Each layer of the forest has its own kinds of plants and animals. Some animals live all their lives in one layer; others move between layers.

At the top of a rain forest are the emergents. These tall trees stick up, here and there, above the other trees. Eagles nest in emergents. They look down into the lower treetops below to spot monkeys, birds, and sloths. Then they swoop down to catch their meals.

The leafy tops of the next-tallest trees form a layer called the canopy. Leaves, fruit, flowers, seeds, and nuts that grow in the canopy provide food for many animals. In South American rain forests, parrots, macaws, and toucans soar from tree to tree in search of fruit and nuts. Sloths are slow, furry animals that hang from branches. They eat leaves and fruit. Monkeys can be found in almost every rain forest. They swing through the canopy, using their long limbs and tails. In Asian rain forests, large bats called flying foxes sail from tree to tree in search of fruit. Plants such as moss, orchids, and bromeliads grow on trees. Some bromeliads in South America have leaves that form cups that catch water. Many animals drink from these plants.

The understory is the layer below the canopy. It is shadowy, and the plants found here include ferns, palms, and shrubs. These plants can survive in dim light. Birds in the understory fly short distances from branch to branch. Many have small wings but strong legs for climbing. Tree frogs also move about, using suction cups on their toes that help them stick to the trees.

The bottom layer, the forest floor, is quite dark. Here are fallen fruits, flowers, and twigs. These provide some nutrients to the soil for the few plants that live here. Many insects live here, as well as some large animals. Tapirs, which are somewhat like pigs, use their long snouts to tear off leaves to eat. Jaguars, which live in Central and South American rain forests, hunt tapirs and rodents.

Reading Time _____

Recalling Facts

1. The emergents are
   - ❏ a. eagles in a rain forest.
   - ❏ b. the tallest trees in a rain forest.
   - ❏ c. bromeliads.

2. Fruit, nuts, and seeds that grow _____ provide food for many animals.
   - ❏ a. in the emergents
   - ❏ b. in the canopy
   - ❏ c. on the forest floor

3. A rain forest plant that holds rain water in its leaves is a
   - ❏ a. fern.
   - ❏ b. bromeliad.
   - ❏ c. coconut palm.

4. The understory has
   - ❏ a. bright light.
   - ❏ b. dim light.
   - ❏ c. no light.

5. Jaguars can be found in
   - ❏ a. southern Africa.
   - ❏ b. Southeast Asia.
   - ❏ c. Central and South America.

Understanding Ideas

6. One can infer from the article that the tropical rain forest biome is important mainly because
   - ❏ a. many young people are interested in it.
   - ❏ b. its plants and animals are very beautiful.
   - ❏ c. it has conditions that are not found in other biomes.

7. One can conclude from reading this article that different animals live in different layers of the rain forest because
   - ❏ a. smaller animals can climb higher than larger animals.
   - ❏ b. each animal blends in with a different surrounding.
   - ❏ c. each layer provides different living conditions.

8. It is likely that there are few plants on the forest floor because
   - ❏ a. the forest floor is crowded with hungry animals.
   - ❏ b. the soil is too wet for most kinds of plants.
   - ❏ c. it is dark there.

9. One can conclude from the article that animals in the rain forest spend most of their time
   - ❏ a. warming themselves in the sun.
   - ❏ b. finding food.
   - ❏ c. taking care of their children.

10. Another example of a biome is
    - ❏ a. a desert.
    - ❏ b. Mars.
    - ❏ c. California.

Tropical rain forests contain a greater diversity of plants and animals than any other biome. Rain forests also provide rubber, lumber, nuts, fruit, rice, coffee, tea, spices, and medicines. But rain forests are being destroyed at a rapid rate. As populations increase, forestland is being cleared for farms. As a result, some species of plants and animals that are found only in tropical rain forests are now threatened with extinction.

Rain-forest soil is low in nutrients, and so farmers cannot use the same land for very long. Sometimes they must cut down another section of forest every three or four years. Animals and plants die out. Sometimes people capture wild parrots and iguanas and sell them to smugglers who take them to other countries.

Much is being done to solve these problems. Groups and governments are working to set aside rain forest land as nature reserves. Schools, clubs, and companies in different parts of the world are raising money to help buy the land. Some rain forests are being managed. Trees are cut down only in small areas. This lets the rain forest heal itself. The development of better farming methods means that the same land can be reused. And some countries have passed laws that make it illegal to trap and sell wild animals.

1. **Recognizing Words in Context**

   Find the word *diversity* in the passage. One definition below is closest to the meaning of that word. One definition has the opposite or nearly opposite meaning. The remaining definition has a completely different meaning. Label the definitions C for *closest*, O for *opposite or nearly opposite*, and D for *different*.

   _____ a. variety

   _____ b. sameness

   _____ c. group

2. **Distinguishing Fact from Opinion**

   Two of the statements below present *facts*, which can be proved correct. The other statement is an *opinion*, which expresses someone's thoughts or beliefs. Label the statements F for *fact* and O for *opinion*.

   _____ a. Some tropical rain forests are quickly being destroyed.

   _____ b. Some medicines come from rain forest plants.

   _____ c. Rain forests are more important than farms.

3. Keeping Events in Order

Label the statements below 1, 2, and 3 to show the order in which the events happen.

_____ a. Crops can no longer be grown on the land.

_____ b. People clear forestland for farming.

_____ c. Nutrients in the soil are used up.

4. Making Correct Inferences

Two of the statements below are correct *inferences*, or reasonable guesses. They are based on information in the passage. The other statement is an incorrect, or faulty, inference. Label the statements C for *correct* inference and F for *faulty* inference.

_____ a. There is a shortage of farmland in some countries that have rain forests.

_____ b. It takes a long time for rain forest plants to grow back once land has been cleared.

_____ c. Soon all rain forest plants and animals will be safe from extinction.

5. Understanding Main Ideas

One of the statements below expresses the main idea of the passage. One statement is too general, or too broad. The other explains only part of the passage; it is too narrow. Label the statements M for *main idea*, B for *too broad*, and N for *too narrow*.

_____ a. Tropical rain forests have been disappearing rapidly.

_____ b. Smugglers are helping remove lizards and birds from rain forests.

_____ c. Tropical rain forests make up a unique biome.

Correct Answers, Part A _____

Correct Answers, Part B _____

Total Correct Answers _____

COMPREHENSION SCORE

Put an X on the line above each lesson number to indicate your total correct answers and comprehension score for that lesson.

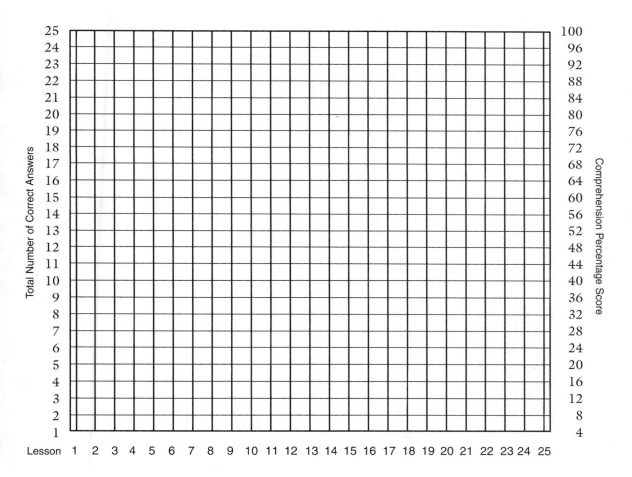

COMPREHENSION SKILLS PROFILE

Put an X in the box above each question type to indicate an incorrect reponse to any part of that question.

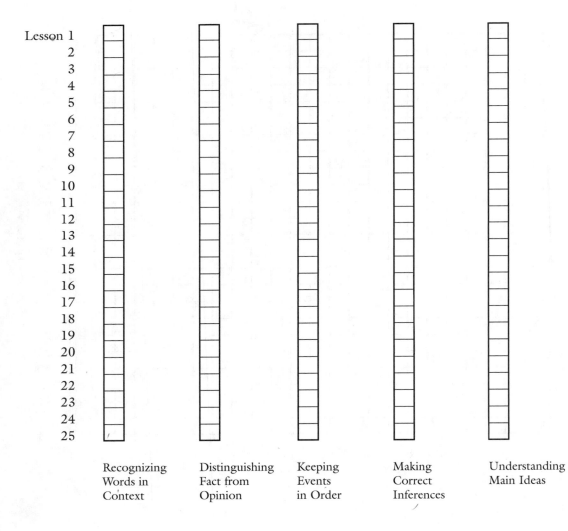

Lesson	Recognizing Words in Context	Distinguishing Fact from Opinion	Keeping Events in Order	Making Correct Inferences	Understanding Main Ideas
1					
2					
3					
4					
5					
6					
7					
8					
9					
10					
11					
12					
13					
14					
15					
16					
17					
18					
19					
20					
21					
22					
23					
24					
25					